History of California

Helen Elliott Bandini

Contents

HISTORY OF CALIFORNIA

BY

Helen Elliott Bandini

Preface

This book is an attempt to present the history of California in so simple and interesting a way that children may read it with pleasure. It does not confine itself to the history of one section or period, but tells the story of all the principal events from the Indian occupancy through the Spanish and Mission days, the excitement of the gold discovery, the birth of the state, down to the latest events of yesterday and to-day. Several chapters, also, are devoted to the development of California's great industries. The work is designed not only for children, but also for older people interested in the story of California, including the tourists who visit the state by the thousand every year.

For her information the writer has depended almost entirely upon source material, seldom making use of a secondary work. Her connection with the old Spanish families has opened to her unusual advantages for the study of old manuscripts and for the gathering of recollections of historical events which she has taken from the lips of aged Spanish residents, always verifying a statement before using it. She has, also, from long familiarity with the Spanish-speaking people, been able to interpret truly the life of the Spanish and Mission period.

The illustrator of the history, Mr. Roy J. Warren, has made a careful study of the manuscript, chapter by chapter. He has also been a faithful student of California and her conditions; his illustrations are, therefore, in perfect touch with the text and are as true to facts as the history itself.

The thanks of the author are due not only to a host of writers from whom she has gained valuable assistance, and some of whose names are among those in the references at the end of the book, but to others to whom further acknowledgment is due. First of these is Professor H. Morse Stephens, whose suggestions from the inception of the work until its completion have been of incalculable advantage, and whose generous offer to read the proof sheets crowns long months of friendly interest. Secondly, the author is indebted to the faithful and constant supervision of her sister, Miss Agnes Elliott of the Los Angeles State Normal School, without whose wide experience as a teacher of history and economics the work could never have reached its present plane. The author also offers her thanks to Mr. Charles F. Lummis, to whom not only she but all students of California history must ever be indebted; to Mrs. Mary M. Coman, Miss Isabel Frazee, to the officers of the various state departments, especially Mr. Lewis E. Aubrey, State Mineralogist, and Mr. Thomas J. Kirk and his assistant Mr. Job Wood of the educational department; to Miss Nellie Rust, Librarian of the Pasadena City Library, and her corps of accommodating and intelligent assistants, and to the librarians of the Los Angeles City Library and State Normal School.

The passages from the Century Magazine quoted in Chapters V-IX are inserted by express permission of the publishers, the Century Company. Acknowledgment is due, also, to the publishers of the Overland Monthly for courtesy in permitting the use of copyright material; and to D. Appleton & Co. for permission to insert selections from Sherman's Memoirs.

Chapter I.
The Land and the Name

Once upon a time, about four hundred years ago, there was published in old Spain a novel which soon became unusually popular. The successful story of those days was one which caught the fancy of the men, was read by them, discussed at their gatherings, and often carried with them when they went to the wars or in search of adventures. This particular story would not interest readers of to-day save for this passage: "Know that on the right hand of the Indies there is an island called California, very near the Terrestrial Paradise, and it is peopled by black women who live after the fashion of Amazons. This island is the strongest in the world, with its steep rocks and great cliffs, and there is no metal in the island but gold."

There is no doubt that some bold explorer, crossing over from Spain to Mexico and enlisting under the leadership of the gallant Cortez, sailed the unknown South Sea (the Pacific) and gave to the new land discovered by one of Cortez's pilots the name of the golden island in this favorite story.

This land, thought to be an island, is now known to us as the peninsula of Lower California. The name first appeared in 1542 on the map of Domingo Castillo, and was soon applied to all the land claimed by Spain from Cape San Lucas up the coast as far north as 441, which was probably a little higher than any Spanish explorer had ever sailed.

"Sir Francis Drake," says the old chronicle, "was the first Englishman to sail on the back side of America," and from that time until now California has been considered the back door of the country. This was natural because the first settlements in the United States were along the Atlantic seacoast. The people who came from England kept their faces turned eastward, looking to the Mother Country for help, and watching Europe, and later England herself, as a quarter from which danger might come, as indeed it did in the war of the Revolution and that of 1812.

During the last few years, however, various events have happened to change this attitude. Through its success in the late Spanish war the United States gained confidence in its own powers, while the people of the old world began to realize that the young republic of the western hemisphere, since it did not hesitate to make war in the interests of humanity, would not be apt to allow its own rights to be imposed upon. The coming of the Philippine and Hawaiian Islands under the protection of the United States, the Russo-Japanese war, which opened the eyes of the world to the strength of Japan and the wisdom of securing its trade, and the action of the United States in undertaking the building of the Panama Canal, are indications that the Pacific will in the future support a commerce the greatness of which we of to-day cannot estimate. With danger from European interference no longer pressing closely upon the nation, President Roosevelt in 1907 took a decided step in recognizing the importance of the Pacific when he sent to that coast so large a number of the most modern vessels of the navy. In fact, the nation may now be said to have faced about, California becoming the front door of our country.

It is well, then, to ask ourselves what we know about the state which is to form part of the reception room of one of the leading nations of the world.

It is a long strip of territory, bounded on one side by the ocean so well named Pacific, which gives freshness and moisture to the ever-blowing westerly winds.

On the other side is a mountain range, one thousand miles long, with many of its peaks covered with perpetual snow, holding in its lofty arms hundreds of ice-cold lakes, its sides timbered with the most wonderful forests of the world.

Few regions of the same size have so great a range of altitude as California, some portions of its desert lands being below sea level, while several of its mountains are over ten thousand feet in height. In its climate, too, there are wide differences as regards heat and cold, although its coast lands, whether north or south, are much more temperate than the corresponding latitudes on the Atlantic coast. The difference in the climate of the northern and southern portions of the state is more marked in the matter of moisture. Most of the storms of California have their beginning out in the North Pacific Ocean. They travel in a southeasterly direction, striking the coast far to the north in summer, but in winter extending hundreds of miles farther south. During November, December, January, and February they often reach as far south as the Mexican line. Then, only, does southern California have rain. The water necessary for use in the summer time is gained by irrigation from the mountain streams, which are supplied largely from the melting snows on the Sierras.

The home lands of the state may be divided into two portions: the beautiful border country rising from the Pacific in alternate valleys and low rolling foothills to the edge of the Coast Range; and the great central valley or basin, which lies like a vast pocket almost entirely encircled by mountains the high Sierras on the east, on the west the low Coast Range. Two large rivers with their tributaries drain this valley: the San Joaquin, flowing from the south; and the Sacramento, flowing from the north. Joining near the center of the state, they cut their way through the narrow passage, the Strait of Carquinez, and casting their waters into the beautiful Bay of San Francisco, finally reach the ocean through the Golden Gate.

Down from the Sierras, mighty glaciers carried the soil for this central valley, grinding and pulverizing it as it was rolled slowly along. Many years this process continued. The rain, washing the mountain sides, brought its tribute in the rich soil and decayed vegetation of the higher region, until a natural seed bed was formed, where there can be raised in abundance a wonderful variety of plants and trees. In the coast valleys the soil is alluvial, the fine washing of mountain rocks; this is mixed in some places with a warmer, firmer loam and in others with a gravelly soil, which is the best known for orange raising.

The state owes much to her mountains, for not only have they contributed to her fertile soil, but they hold in their rocky slopes the gold and silver mines which have transformed the whole region from an unknown wilderness to a land renowned for its riches and beauty. They lift their lofty peaks high in the air like mighty strongholds, and, shutting out the desert winds, catch the clouds as they sail in from the ocean, making them pay heavy tribute in fertilizing rain to the favored land below.

The climate, which of all the precious possessions of California is the most valuable, is best described by Bret Harte in the lines, "Half a year of clouds and flowers; half a year of dust and sky." Either half is enjoyable, for in the summer, or dry season, fogs or delightful westerly winds soon moderate a heated spell, and in nearly all parts of the state the nights are cool; while the rainy, or winter season, changes to balmy springtime as soon as the storm is over.

In a large portion of the state the climate is such that the inhabitants may spend much of their time out of doors. As a rule few duties are attended to in the house which can possibly be performed in the open air. It is growing to be more and more the custom to have, in connection with a Californian home, a tent bedroom where the year round one or more of the members of the family sleep, with only a wall of canvas between them and nature.

The vacation time is spent largely in summer camps, at either mountain or seashore, or, quite often, a pleasant party of one or two families live together, very simply, under the greenwood tree beside some spring or stream, spending a few weeks in gypsy fashion. While the young folk grow sturdy and beautiful, the older members of the party become filled with strength and a joy of living which helps them through the cares and struggles of the rest of the year. This joy in outdoor life is not, however, a discovery of to-day. The old Spanish families spent as much time as possible in the courtyard, the house being deserted save at night. When upon journeys, men, women, and children slept in the open air. Even the clothes-washing period was turned into a kind of merrymaking. Whole families joined together to spend days in the vicinity of some stream, where they picnicked while the linen was being cleansed in the running water and dried on the bushes near by.

Once before, when the world was younger, there was a land similar to this,-- sea-kissed, mountain-guarded, with such gentle climate and soft skies. Its people, who also lived much out of doors at peace with nature, became almost perfect in health and figure, with mental qualities which enabled them to give to the world the best it has known in literature and art. What the ancient Greeks were, the people of California may become; but with an advancement in knowledge and loving-kindness of man toward man which heathen Athens never knew.

What will be the result of this outdoor life cannot yet be told; climate has always had an active influence in shaping the character and type of a people. With a climate mild and healthful, yet bracing; with a soil so rich that the touch of irrigation makes even the sandiest places bloom with the highest beauty of plant, tree, and vine; with an ocean warm and gentle, and skies the kindliest in the world,-- there is, if we judge by the lesson history teaches, a promise of a future for California greater and more noble than the world has yet known.

Chapter II.
The Story of the Indians

"Run, Cleeta, run, the waves will catch you." Cleeta scudded away, her naked little body shining like polished mahogany. She was fleet of foot, but the incoming breakers from the bosom of the great Pacific ran faster still; and the little Indian girl was caught in its foaming water, rolled over and over, and cast upon the sandy beach, half choked, yet laughing with the fun of it.

"Foolish Cleeta, you might have been drowned; that was a big wave. What made you go out so far?" said Gesnip, the elder sister.

"I found such a lot of mussels, great big ones, I wish I could go back and get them," said the little one, looking anxiously at the water.

"The waves are coming in higher and higher and it is growing late," said Gesnip; "besides, I have more mussels already than you and I can well carry. The boys have gone toward the river mouth for clams. They will be sure to go home the other way."

Cleeta ran to the basket and looked in.

"I should think there were too many for us to carry," she said, as she tried with all her strength to lift it by the carry straps. "What will you do with them; throw some back into the water?"

"No, I don't like to do that," answered her sister, frowning, "for it has been so long since we have had any. The wind and the waves have been too high for us to gather any. Look, Cleeta, look; what are those out on the water? I do believe they are boats."

"No," said the little girl; "I see what you mean, but boats never go out so far as that."

"Not tule boats," said Gesnip, "but big thick one made out of trees; that is the kind they have at Santa Catalina, the island where uncle lives. It has been a long time since he came to see us, not since you were four years old, but mother is always looking for him."

The children gazed earnestly seaward at a fleet of canoes which were making for the shore. "Do you think it is uncle?" asked Cleeta.

"Yes," replied her sister, uncertainly, "I think it may be." Then, as the sunlight struck full on the boats "Yes, yes, I am sure of it, for one is red, and no on else has a boat of that color; all others are brown."

"Mother said he would bring abalone when he came," cried Cleeta, dancing from one foot to the other; "and she said they are better than mussels or anything else for soup."

"He will bring fish," said Gesnip, "big shining fish with yellow tails."

"Mother said he would bring big blue ones with hard little seams down their sides," said Cleeta.

Meantime the boats drew nearer. They were of logs hollowed out until they were fairly light, but still seeming too clumsy for safe seagoing craft. In each were several men. One sat in the stern and steered, the others knelt in pairs, each man helping propel the boat by means of a stick some four feet long, more like a pole than a paddle, which he worked with great energy over the gunwale.

"I am afraid of them," said Cleeta, drawing close to her sister. "They do not look like the people I have seen. Their faces are the color of the kah-hoom mother weaves in her baskets. There are only three like us, and they all have such strange clothes."

"Do not be afraid," said Gesnip. "I see uncle; he is one of the dark ones like ourselves. The island people have yellow skins."

The time was the year 1540, and the people, the Californians of that day. The men in the boat were mostly from the island of Santa Catalina, and were fairer, with more regular features, than the inhabitants of the mainland, who in southern California were a short, thick-set race, with thick lips, dark brown skin, coarse black hair, and eyes small and shining like jet-black beads. They were poorly clothed in winter; in summer a loin cloth was often all that the men wore, while the children went naked a large part of the year.

With wonderful skill the badly shaped boats were guided safely over the breakers until their bows touched the sand. Then the men leaped out and, half wading, half swimming, pulled them from the water and ran them up on the beach.

The little girls drew near and stood quietly by, waiting to be spoken to. Presently the leading man, who was short, dark, and handsomely dressed in a suit of sealskin ornamented with abalone shell, turned to them.

"Who are these little people?" he asked, in a kind voice.

"We are the children of Cuchuma and Macana," replied Gesnip, working her toes in and out of the soft sand, too shy to look her uncle in the face.

"Children of my sister, Sholoc is glad to see you," said the chief, laying his hand gently on Cleeta's head. "Your mother, is she well?"

"She is well and looking for you these many moons," said Gesnip.

The men at once began unloading the boats. The children watched the process with great interest, Abalone in their shells, a dainty prized then as well as now, fish, yellowtail and bonito, filled to the brim the large baskets which the men slung to their backs, carrying them by means of a strap over the forehead. On their heads they placed ollas, or water jars, of serpentine from quarries which may be seen in Santa Catalina to-day, the marks of the tools of workmen of, that time still in the rocks.

There were also strings of bits of abalone shell which had been punctured and then polished, and these Sholoc hung around his neck.

"Uncle," exclaimed Gesnip, touching one of these strings, "how much money! You have grown rich at Santa Catalina. What will you buy?"

"Buy me a wife, perhaps," was the reply. "I will give two strings for a good wife. Do you know any worth so much?"

"No," said the girl, stoutly. "I don't know any worth two whole strings of abalone. You can get a good wife for much less."

The men, who had succeeded in loading the contents of the boats on their heads and backs, now marched away, in single file, crossing the heavy sand dunes slowly, then mounting the range of foothills beyond. The children followed. Gesnip had her basket bound to her head by a strap round her forehead; but, though her uncle had taken out part of the contents, it was a heavy load for the child.

As they neared the top of the hill, Sholoc, who was ahead, lifted his hand and motioned them to stop.

"Hush," he said softly, "elk." Swiftly the men slipped off their loads and with bows in hand each one crept flat on his belly over the hill crest. Gesnip and Cleeta peeped through the high grass. Below them was a wide plain, dotted with clumps of bushes, and scattered over it they could see a great herd of elk, whose broad, shining antlers waved above the grass and bushes upon which they were feeding.

"Are those elk too?" asked Cleeta, presently, pointing toward the foothills at their left.

"No," replied her sister, "I think those are antelope. I like to see them run. How funny their tails shake. But watch the men; they are going to shoot."

As she spoke, four of the hunters, who had crept well up toward the game, rose to their feet, holding their bows horizontally, not perpendicularly. These weapons, which were made of cedar wood, were about four feet in length, painted at the ends black or dark blue, the middle, which was almost two inches broad, being wrapped with elk sinew. The strings also were of sinew. The quiver which each man carried at his side was made from the skin of a wild cat or of a coyote. A great hunter like Sholoc might make his quiver from the tails of lions he had killed. Projecting from the quiver were the bright-feathered ends of the arrows, which were of reed and were two or three feet long, with points of bone, flint, or obsidian.

The hunters, knowing how hard it was to kill large game, had chosen their arrows carefully, taking those that had obsidian points. Almost at the same moment they let fly their shafts. Three elk leaped into the air. One tumbled over in a somersault which broke one of its antlers, and then lay dead, shot through the heart by Sholoc. Another took a few leaps, but a second arrow brought it to its knees. Then it sank slowly over upon its side; but it struck so fiercely at the hunter who ran up to kill it with his horn knife that he drew back and shot it again.

"Where is the third elk?" asked Cleeta, looking around.

"Over there," said Gesnip, pointing across the plain.

"Then they have lost it," said the child, with disappointment.

"No, I think not. It is wounded. I saw the blood on its side," said the sister. "See, one of the men is following it, and it is half a mile behind the herd. I am sure he will get it."

"This has been a lucky day," said Gesnip. "So much food. Our stomachs will not ache with hunger for a long time."

"That is because mother wove a game basket to Chinigchinich so he would send food," said Cleeta.

By the time the party had traveled two miles, Gesnip, with her load, and Cleeta, whose bare brown legs were growing very tired, lagged behind.

"O dear," said the elder sister, "we shall surely be too late to go into camp with uncle." Just then a whoop sounded behind them, and a boy of thirteen, dressed in a rabbit-skin shirt, carrying a bow in his hand, came panting up to them.

"Payuchi," said Gesnip, eagerly, "carry my basket for me and I will tell you some good news."

"No," replied Payuchi, shaking his head, "it is a girl's place to carry the basket."

"Just this little way, and it is such good news" urged Gesnip. "It will, make your heart glad."

"Very well, then, tell it quickly," said the boy, changing the basket of mussels to his own broad back.

"Sholoc has come from Santa Catalina with baskets of abalone and fish, and with ollas all speckled, and strings of money. He is near the top of the grade now. Upon hearing the good news the lad darted away at a great pace, his sisters following as fast as they could. Sholoc and his party had stopped to rearrange their loads, so the children overtook them at the head of the trail leading to their home.

"Below them was a valley dotted with live oaks, and along the banks of the stream that ran through it was a thick growth of alders, sycamores, and willows. At the foot of the trail, near the water, was a cluster of what looked like low, round straw stacks. No straw stacks were they, however, but houses, the only kind of homes known in southern California at that time.

"It was the Indian settlement where Gesnip, Cleeta, and Payuchi lived, and of which their father, Cuchuma, was chief. The jacals, or wigwams, were made of long willow boughs, driven into the ground closely in a circle, the ends bent over and tied together with deer sinews. They were covered with a thatching of grass that, when dry, made them look like straw stacks.

"Sholoc stepped to the-edge of the bluff and gave a long, quavering cry which could be heard far in the still evening air. Instantly out of the group of jacals came a crowd of men and boys, who gave answering cries."

"I am glad they have a fire," said Cleeta, as she saw the big blaze in the middle of the settlement, "I am so cold."

"Take my hand and let's run," said Gesnip, and partly running and partly sliding, they followed the men of the party, who, notwithstanding their heavy loads, were trotting down the steep trail.

They were met at the foot of the grade by a crowd which surrounded them, all chattering at once. Sholoc told of the elk, and a number of men started off on the run to bring in the big game. As the visitors entered camp, Macana, a kind-faced woman, better dressed than most of her tribe, came forward. She placed her hand on Sholoc's shoulder, her face lighting up with love and happiness.

"You are welcome, brother," she said.

"The sight of you is good to my eyes, sister," an answered Sholoc. That was all the greeting, although the two loved each other well. Macana took the basket from Payuchi's back.

"Come," she called to Gesnip, "and help me wash the mussels." Then, as she saw the younger girl shivering as she crouched over the fire, "Cleeta, you need not be cold any longer; your rabbit skin dress is done. Go into the jacal and put it on." Cleeta obeyed with dancing eyes.

Gesnip followed her mother to the stream.

"Take this," said Macana, handing her an openwork net or bag, "and hold it while I empty in some of the mussels. Now lift them up and down in the water to wash out the sand. That will do; put them into this basket, and I will give you some more."

Meantime some of the women had taken a dozen or more fish from Sholoc's baskets, and removing their entrails with bone knives, wrapped them in many thicknesses of damp grass and laid them in the hot ashes and coals to bake.

When the mussels were all cleaned, Macana emptied them into a large basket half filled with water, and threw in a little acorn meal and a handful of herbs. Then, using two green sticks for tongs, she drew out from among the coals some smooth gray stones which had become very hot. Brushing these off with a bunch of tules, she lifted them by means of a green stick having a loop in the end which fitted round the stones, flinging them one by one into the basket in which were the mussels and water. Immediately the water, heated by the stones, began to boil, and when the soup was ready, she set the basket down beside her own jacal and called her children to her. Payuchi, Gesnip, Cleeta, and their little four-year-old brother, Nakin, gathered about the basket, helping themselves with abalone shells, the small holes of which their mother had plugged with wood.

"Isn't father going to have some first?" asked Payuchi, before they began the meal.

"Not this time; he will eat with Sholoc and the men when the fish are ready," replied his mother.

"This is good soup," said Gesnip. "I am glad I worked hard before the water came up. But, Payuchi, didn't you and Nopal get any clams?"

"Yes," said her brother, making a face; he had dipped down where the stones were hottest and the soup thickest, and had taken a mouthful that burned him. "Yes, we got some clams, more than I could carry; but Nopal was running races with the other boys and would not come, so I left him to bring them. He will lose his fish dinner if he doesn't hurry."

"Mother," said Cleeta, "may we stay up to the fish bake?"

"No," answered her mother. "You and Nakin must go to bed, but I will save some for your breakfast. You are tired, Cleeta."

"Yes, I am tired," said the little girl, leaning her head against her mother's shoulder, "but I am warm in my rabbit-skin dress. We all have warm dresses now. Please tell me a good-night story," she begged. "We have been good and brought in much food."

"Yes, tell us how the hawk and coyote made the sun," said Gesnip.

"Very well," said the mother, "only you must be quite still."

"It was in the beginning of all things, and a bowl of darkness, blacker than the pitch lining of our water basket, covered the earth. Man, when he would go abroad, fell against man, against trees, against wild animals, even against Lollah, the bear, who would, in turn, hug the unhappy one to death. Birds flying in the air came together and fell struggling to the earth. All was confusion."

"Once the hawk, by chance, flew in the face of the coyote. Instead of fighting about it as naughty children might, they, like people of good manners, apologized many times. Then they talked over the unhappy state of things and determined to remedy the evil. The coyote first gathered a great heap of dried tules, rolled them together into a ball, and gave them to the hawk, with some pieces of flint. The hawk, taking them in his talons, flew straight up into the sky, where he struck fire with his flints, lit the ball of reeds, and left it there whirling along with a bright yellow light, as it continues to whirl to-day; for it, children, is our sun, ruler of the day."

"The hawk next flew back for another ball to rule the night, but the coyote had no tule gathered, and the hawk hurried him so that some damp stems were mixed in. The hawk flew with this ball into the sky and set it afire but because of the green tules it burned with only a dim light; and this, children, is our moon, ruler of the night."

"That is a fine story," said Payuchi. "I am glad I did not live when there was no light."

"Tell us how the coyote danced with the star," said Gesnip.

"No," replied the mother, "another time we shall see. Now I shall sing to coax sleep to tired eyes, and the little ones will go to bed." And this was what she sang: "Pah-high-nui-veve, veve, veve, shumeh, veve, veve, veve, shumeh, Pah-high-nui-veve," and so on, repeating these words over and over until Cleeta and Nakin were sound asleep. Then she laid them on their tule mats, which were spread on the floor of the jacal, where baby Nahal, close wrapped in his cocoon-shaped cradle, had been a long time sleeping.

"Mother," said Gesnip, coming into the jacal, "they have brought in the elk. Don't you want something from them?"

"Yes," replied Macana, "I will go and see about it. I want one of the skins to make your father a warm hunting dress."

The Indians who had gone after the elk had skinned and cut them up where they lay, as they were so large that the burden had to be distributed among a number of carriers. Macana found Sholoc busy portioning out parts of the elk. As he had a fine seal-skin suit himself, he gladly gave her the skin of the deer which he had shot.

"Isn't that a big one?" said Payuchi. "It will make father a fine hunting suit, it is so thick." Gesnip was loaded down with some of the best cuts of the meat to take to her father's jacal. Cuchuma himself began removing the tendons from the legs, to cure for bowstrings, and to wrap a new bow he was going to make.

"Here, Nopal," said Sholoc to his oldest nephew, a lad of fifteen, "I will give you a piece of the antler and you can grind it down and make yourself a hunting knife. It is time you ceased to play and became a hunter. I had killed much game when I was your age."

"Will you give me some of the brains that I may finish tanning a deerskin? I have been waiting to finish it until I could get some brains, but it has been a long time since any one has brought in big game," said Macana.

"Yes," answered Sholoc, "you shall have them. Payuchi, hand me my elk-horn ax so that I can split open the head, and you can take the brains to the jacal." Soon not a piece of meat, a bit of skin, tendon, or bone, was left. All was put to use by these people of the forest. And now the feast was ready. The women had roasted many pieces of elk's meat over the coals. The fish had been taken from under the hot ashes, the half burned grass removed from around them, and the fish broken into pieces and put in flat baskets shaped like platters. There were also pieces of elk meat and cakes of acorn meal baked on hot stones.

As was the custom with the Indians, the men were served first. Payuchi watched anxiously as his father and the other men took large helpings from the baskets.

"Do you think there will be enough for us to have any?" he asked Gesnip. "I am so hungry and they are eating so much. If I were a man, I should remember about the women and children."

"No; you wouldn't if you were a man; men never do," answered Gesnip. "But you need not worry, there is plenty. Mother said there would be some left for breakfast."

"Wait for that till I get through," said Payuchi, laughing. After all had eaten a hearty meal, more than for many weeks they had been able to have at any one time, the tired women each gathered her children together and took them to her own jacal, leaving the men sitting around the camp fire. Payuchi, who tumbled to sleep as soon as his head touched his sleeping mat, was wakened by some one pulling his rabbit-skin coat, which he wore nights as well as days.

"Payuchi," said a voice, "wake up."

"I have not been asleep," answered the boy, stoutly, as he rubbed his eyes to get them open. "What do you want, Nopal?" for he saw his brother speaking to him.

"Hush, do not waken mother," said Nopal, speaking very softly. "I know that the men will make an offering to Chinigchinich. I am going to watch them. We are old enough, at least I am. Do you want to come?"

A star shone in at the top of the jacal, and Payuchi gazed up at it, blinking, while he pulled his thoughts together.

"They will punish us if they find us out," said he at length.

"But we won't let them find us out, stupid one," replied his brother, impatiently.

"What if Chinigchinich should be angry with us? He does not like to have children in the ceremony of the offering," said Payuchi.

"I will give him my humming-bird skin, and you shall give him your mountain quail head; then he will be pleased with us," answered Nopal.

"All right," said the boy; "I do not like very well to part with that quail head, but perhaps it is a good thing to do."

Creeping softly from the jacal, the boys crouched in the shade of a willow bush and watched the men by the camp fire.

"They are standing up. They are just going," said Payuchi, "and every one has something in his hand. Father has two bows; I wonder why."

"I think he is going to make an offering of the new bow to Chinigchinich," answered Nopal. "I thought he was going to keep it and give me his old one," he added, with some disappointment.

"What are they offering for?" asked the young brother.

"For rain," said Nopal. "See, they are going now." In single file the men walked swiftly away, stepping so softly that not a twig cracked.

After a little the boys followed, slipping from bush to bush that they might not be discovered. They had walked about a mile, when they came to thicker woods with bigger trees and saw a light ahead of them. Nopal laid his hand on his brother to stop him. Peeping through a scrub-oak bush, they looked down into a little glade arched over with great live oaks. In the middle of the opening they saw, by the light of a low fire, a small cone-shaped hut. Beside it stood a gigantic figure painted and adorned with shells, feathers, rattlesnake skins, and necklaces of bone.

"Come back," whispered Payuchi, his teeth chattering with fear. "It is Chinigchinich himself; he will see us, and we shall die."

"No," answered Nopal, "it is only Nihie, the medicine man. He looks so tall because of his headdress. It is made of framework of dried tules covered with feathers and fish bladders. I saw it one day in his jacal, and it is as tall as I am. That jacal beside him is the vanquech [temple], and I think there is something awful there. You see if there isn't. Hush, now! Squat down. Here they come."

In a procession the men came into the opening, and, stalking solemnly by, each cast down at the door of the temple an offering of some object which he prized. Cuchuma gave a bone knife which he greatly valued, and a handsome new bow. Sholoc gave a speckled green stone olla from Santa Catalina and a small string of money; but these were chiefs' offerings. The other gifts were simpler--shells, acorn meal, baskets, birds' skins, but always something for which the owner cared.

At last the medicine man, satisfied with the things offered which became his own when the ceremony was over, stooped and drew forth the sacred emblem from the temple. It was not even an idol, only a fetich composed of a sack made from the skin of a coyote, the head carefully preserved and stuffed, while the body was dressed smooth of hair and adorned with hanging shells and tufts of birds' feathers. A bundle of arrows protruded from the open mouth, giving it a fierce appearance. While Nihie held it up, the men circled round once again, this time more rapidly, and as they passed the medicine man, each gave a spring into the air, shooting an arrow upward with all his force. When the last man had disappeared under the trees, Nihie replaced the skin in the temple, put out the fire, and, singing a kind of chant, he led the men back to their jacals. The boys stood up. Payuchi shivered and drew a long breath.

"We must get away now; Nihie will be back soon to get the offerings," said Nopal.

"But first we must offer our gifts, or Chinigchinich will be angry," said Payuchi.

"Come on, then," said the brother; so, stealing softly down the hillside, the boys cast their offerings on the pile in front of the hut and ran away, taking a roundabout path home, that they might not meet the medicine man returning.

"We must hurry to get in the jacal before father," said Nopal, suddenly. "I didn't think of that. Run, Payuchi, run faster." But they were in time after all, and were stretched out on their mats some minutes before their father and Sholoc came in.

Macana's first duty in the morning was to attend to the baby, whose wide-open black eyes gave the only sign that it was awake. She unfastened it from the basket and unwrapped it, rubbing the little body over with its morning bath of grease until the firm skin shone as if varnished. When it had nursed and was comfortable, she put the little one back in its cradle basket, which she leaned up against the side of the hut, where the little prisoner might see all that was going on.

Instead of the usual breakfast of acorn meal mush, the children had a plentiful meal of fish which their mother had saved from the feast of the night before.

"I didn't think any one could catch so many fish as uncle brought last night," said Cleeta, as she helped herself to a piece of yellowtail.

"Yes, they do, though," said Payuchi. "Last night, after supper, uncle told the men some fine stories. I think he has been in places which none of our people have ever seen.

"He told us that once he journeyed many moons toward the land of snow and ice until he came to the country of the Klamath tribe, where he stayed a long time. He said that when they fish they drive posts made of young trees into the bottom of the river and then weave willow boughs in and out until there is a wall of posts and boughs clear across the stream. Then the big red fish come up from the great water into the river. They come, uncle said, so many no one can count them, and the ones behind push against those in front until they are all crowded against the wall, and then the Klamath men catch them with spears and nets until there is food enough for all, and many fish to dry."

"I should like to see that. What else did he tell you?" asked Gesnip.

"He said he visited one place where the great salt water comes into the land and is so big it takes many days to journey round it. Here the people eat fish, clams, and mussels instead of acorns and roots. On the shore they have their feasting ground where they go to eat and dance and tell big stories, and; sometimes to make an of-fering. So many people go there, uncle said, that the shells they have left make a hill, a hill just of shells that is many steps high. From the top of it one may look over the water, which is so long no eye can see the end of it."

"What else did you hear?" asked Gesnip.

"Nothing more, for mother called me," replied her brother. "I should like to hear more of those stories, though."

"Mother," asked Gesnip, as she finished her breakfast, "when am I to begin to braid mats for the new jacal?"

"Soon," replied Macana. "This morning you and Payuchi must gather the tule. Have a large pile when I come home." So saying, the mother strapped the baby on her back and, accompanied by the younger children, went out with other women of the tribe to gather the white acorns from the oaks on the highlands pear the mountains.

The December wind, from the snow-capped peaks, chilled and cut with its icy breath their scantily clothed bodies, but for hours they worked picking up the scattered nuts. The labors of an Indian mother ceased only while she slept.

"Come, Payuchi," said Gesnip, "let us go down to the river and get tules."

"All right," replied the boy, readily. "Sholoc is going down too. He is going to show the men how to make log canoes like his instead of the tule canoes our people use. But I like the tule canoes, because I can use my feet for paddles." When they reached the river, which was really a lagoon or arm of the sea, the children stopped to watch the men at work. A large log, washed down from the mountains by some flood, lay on the bank. It was good hard wood, and the children saw that it was smoking in three places.

"This is going to make two canoes, but neither one will be so big, as uncle's," said Payuchi.

"How can it make two canoes if they burn it up?" asked his sister.

"You are stupid, Gesnip," said her brother. "Don't you see they are burning it to separate it into two parts? Then they will burn each log into the shape of a boat, finishing it up with axes of bone or horn. Uncle told me how they did it."

"Why have they put the green bark on the top of the log?"

"I think it is to keep it from burning along the edge; don't you see? And then there are wider pieces to protect it at the ends. See how they watch the fire and beat it out in one place and then in another."

"Why does it burn so fast?" asked Gesnip.

"Because they have daubed it with pitch. Can't you smell it?" said the boy, sniffing.

"Yes, I can smell it," replied his sister. "But come now and help me gather tules. Father is going to burn down our house and build a new one for winter, and I must make a tule rug for each one of you for beds in the new home. It will take a great many tule stems."

"It is cold to wade," said Payuchi, stepping into the water at the edge of the river.

"Yes," answered Gesnip, "I don't like to gather tules in winter."

The children pulled up the long rough stems one by one until they had a large pile.

"I think we have enough," said Payuchi, after they had been working about two hours.

"Yes, I think so too," said his sister. "My back aches, my hands are sore, and my feet are so cold." Payuchi brought some wild grapevine with which he tied the tule into two bundles, fastening the larger upon his sister's back; for with his people the women and girls were the burden bearers, and a grown Indian would not do any work that his wife could possibly do for him.

After they had traveled a little way on the homeward path, Gesnip stopped.

"Don't go so fast, Payuchi," she begged. "This bundle is so large it nearly tumbles me over."

"Just hurry a little until we get to the foot of the hill yonder where Nopal and the other big boys are playing, and you can rest while I watch the game," answered her brother. Gesnip struggled on, bending under the weight and size of her awkward burden until, with a sigh of relief, she seated herself on a stone to rest while Payuchi, throwing his bundle on the ground, stood up to watch the boys.

"See, Nopal is It," he said. Nopal, coming forward, stooped low and rolled a hoop along the ground, which the boys had pounded smooth and hard for the game.

As the hoop rolled another boy stepped forward and tried to throw a stick through it, but failed. Then all the players pointed their fingers at him and grunted in scorn. Again Nopal rolled the hoop, and this time the boy threw through the ring, and all the boys, and Payuchi too, gave whoops of delight.

The children watched the game until Gesnip said that they must go on, for their mother would be home and want them. When they returned, Macana was warming herself by the fire where the men were sitting.

"See our tule; is it not a great deal?" asked the children, showing their bundles.

"Yes, but not enough," replied their mother. "You will have to go out another day."

The women, who had been working all the morning gathering acorns, now squatted near the fire and began grinding up the nuts which had been already dried.

"Gesnip," called her mother, "bring me the grinding stones." The girl went to the jacal and brought two stones, one a heavy bowlder with a hollow in its top, which had been made partly by stone axes, but more by use; the other stone fitted into this hollow.

"Now bring me the basket of roasted grasshoppers," said the mother. Taking a handful of grasshoppers, Macana put them into the hollow in the larger stone, and with the smaller stone rubbed them to a coarse powder. This powder she put into a small basket which Gesnip brought her.

"I am glad we caught the grasshoppers. They taste better than acorn meal mush," said Payuchi.

"How many grasshoppers there are in the fall," said Gesnip, "and so many rabbits, too."

"We had such a good time at the rabbit drive," said Payuchi.

"And such a big feast afterwards, nearly as good as last night," said Gesnip.

"Tell me about the rabbit drive," said Cleeta, squatting down beside the children in front of the fire.

"It was in the big wash up the river toward the mountains," began Payuchi. "You have seen the rabbits running to hide in a bunch of grass and cactus when you go with mother to the mountains for acorns, haven't you?"

Cleeta nodded. "Not this winter, though. We saw only two to-day," she said.

"That is because of the drive," said her brother. "It was in the afternoon, with the wind blowing from the ocean, and all the men who could shoot best with bow and arrow, or throw the spear well, stood on the other side of the wash."

"Father was there," said Cleeta.

"Yes, and many others," said Payuchi. "Then some of the men and all of us boys got green branches of trees and came down on this side of the wash. Nopal started the fire. It burned along in the grass slowly at first, and when it came too near the jacals on one side or the woods on the other, we would beat it out with the branches, but soon it ran before the wind into the cactus and bunch grass. The rabbits were frightened out and ran from the fire as fast as they could, and in a few minutes they were right at the feet of father and the other hunters. They killed forty before the smoke made them run too."

"My dress was made of their skin," said the little girl, smoothing her gown lovingly. "It keeps me so warm."

"Did the fire burn long?" asked Gesnip.

"No, we beat it out, or it would have gone up the wash into the live oaks; then we boys should have been well punished for our carelessness."

Here their mother called to them.

"Payuchi," she said, "put away this basket of grasshopper meal. And, Gesnip, go to the jacal and find me the coils for basket weaving."

"What shall I bring?" asked Gesnip.

"The large bundle of chippa that is soaking in a basket, and the big coil of yellow kah-hoom and the little one of black tsuwish which are hanging up, and bring me my needle and bone awl."

"Do you want the coil of millay?"

"No, I shall need no red to-day."

Squatted on the ground, where she could feel the warmth of the fire on her back, but where the heat could not dry her basket materials, Macana began her work. Taking a dripping chippa, or willow bough, from the basket where it had been soaking, she dried it on leaves and wound it tightly in a close coil the size of her thumbnail, then spatted it together until it seemed no longer a cord, but a solid piece of wood. Thus she made the base of her basket; then, threading her needle, which was but a horny cactus stem set in a head of hardened pitch, she stitched in and out over the upper and under the lower layer, drawing her thread firmly each time. The thread was the creamy, satin-like kah-hoom. Round and round she coiled the chippa, the butt of one piece overlapping the tip of another, while with her needle she covered all with the smoothly drawn kah-hoom. After a time she laid the kah-hoom aside for a stitch or two of the black root of the tule, called tsuwish.

The children had watched the starting of the basket, then had begun a game of match, with white and black pebbles. After a time Gesnip, looking up from her play, exclaimed, as she saw the black diamond pattern the weaver was making:--

"Mother, why are you weaving a rattlesnake basket?"

"I am making it to please Chinigchinich that he may smile upon me and guard you, children, and Cuchuma from the bite of the rattlesnake. There are so many of them here this year, and I fear for you."

"Thank you, mother," said Gesnip. "If Titas's mother had made a black diamond basket, maybe the snake would not have bitten her."

"I think Chinigchinich does smile upon you," said Payuchi, "for when we were so hungry in the month of roots [October] you wove him the hunting basket with the pattern of deer's antlers, trimmed with quail feathers, and see how much food we have had: first the rabbits, then the grasshoppers, and now the fish and elk."

"While you work tell us how the first baby basket was made," begged Cleeta. The mother nodded; and as she wound and pressed closely the moist chippa, and the cactus needle flew in and out with the creamy kah-hoom or the black tsuwish, she told the story.

"When the mother of all made the basket for the first man child, she used a rainbow for the wood of the back of the basket, with stars woven in each side, and straight lightning down the middle in front. Sunbeams shining on a far-away rain storm formed the fringe in front, where we use strips of buckskin, and the carry straps were brightest sunbeams."

"Mother, you left out that the baby was wrapped in a soft purple cloud from the mountains," said Cleeta.

"Yes, in a purple cloud of evening, wrapped so he could not move leg or arm, but would grow straight and beautiful," said the mother.

For a long while the children watched in silence the patient fingers at their work; then Gesnip asked, "Is it true, mother, that when you were a little child your father and mother and many of your tribe died of hunger?"

"It is true," replied Macana, sadly, "but who told you?"

"Old Cotopacnic, but I thought it was one of his dreams. Why were you all so hungry?" asked the girl.

"Because the rain failed for three seasons. After a time there was no grass, no acorns, the rabbits and deer died or wandered away, the streams dried up so there were no fish, the ground became so dry that there were no more grubs or worms of any kind, no grasshoppers. There was nothing to eat but roots. Nearly all our tribe died, and many other people, too."

"How did you live?" asked Payuchi.

"My aunt had married a chief whose home was in a rich valley in the mountains where it is always green. She came down to see my mother, and when she found how hard it was to get food for us all, she took me by the hand and tumbled

Sholoc who was smaller than little Nakin, into her great seed basket and took us off to the mountains until times should grow better; but the rains did not come until it was too late. I stayed with her until I married your father. Sholoc became a great hunter, then chief of the people of Santa Catalina, where he became a great fisherman also."

The children looked grave.

"Do you think such bad seasons can ever come again?" asked Gesnip.

"Who can tell?" replied the mother, with a sigh. "Last year was very bad and there is little rain yet this year. That is why the men offered gifts to Chinigchinich last night."

"Nobody must take me away from you to keep me from being hungry," said gentle Cleeta, hiding her face in her mother's lap.

"If I were Chinigchinich," said Payuchi, "I would not let so many people die, just because they needed a little more rain. I would not be that kind of a god."

"Hush, my child," said the mother, sternly. "He will hear and punish you. If it is our fate, we must bend to it."

Chapter III
"The Secret of the Strait"

Cabrillo

One afternoon in September, in the year 1542, two broad, clumsy ships, each with the flag of Spain flying above her many sails, were beating their way up the coast of southern California. All day the vessels had been wallowing in the choppy seas, driven about by contrary winds. At last the prow of the leading ship was turned toward shore, where there seemed to be an opening that might lead to a good harbor. At the bow of the ship stood the master of the expedition, the tanned, keen-faced captain, Juan Rodriguez Cabrillo. He was earnestly watching the land before him, which was still some distance away.

"Come hither, Juan," he called to a sturdy lad, about sixteen, who, with an Indian boy, brought from Mexico as interpreter, was also eagerly looking landward. "Your eyes should be better than mine. Think you there is a harbor beyond that point?"

"It surely seems so to me, sir," answered the boy; "and Pepe, whose eyes, you know, are keener than ours, says that he can plainly see the entrance."

"I trust he is right; for this thickening weather promises a storm, and a safe harbor would be a gift of God to us weary ones this night," said the captain, with a sigh.

Since the fair June day when they had sailed out of the harbor on the west shore of Mexico, they had been following first up the coast line of the Peninsula, then of Upper California. No maps or charts of the region showing where lay good harbors or dangerous rocks, could be found in Cabrillo's cabin. Instead, there were maps of this South Sea which pictured terrible dangers for mariners--great whirlpools which could suck down whole fleets of vessels, and immense waterfalls, where it was thought the whole ocean poured off the end of the land into space. A brave man was Captain Cabrillo, for, half believing these stories, he yet sailed steadily on, determined, no matter what happened to himself, to do his duty to the king under whose flag he sailed, and to the viceroy of Mexico, whose funds had furnished the expedition.

California has ever been noted for its brave men, but none have been more courageous than this explorer, who was probably the first white man to set his foot upon its soil. As the ship approached land the crew became silent, every eye being turned anxiously to the opening of the passage which appeared before them. The vessel, driven by the stiff breeze, rushed on, almost touching the rock at one point. Then, caught by a favorable current, it swept into mid-channel, where it moved rapidly forward, until at length it rode safely in the harbor now known as San Diego Bay.

"It is a good port and well inclosed," said Juan Cabrillo, with great satisfaction, gazing out upon the broad sheet of quiet water. "We will name it for our good San Miguel, to whom our prayers for a safe anchorage were offered this morning." Then, when the two ships were riding at anchor, the commander ordered out the boats.

"We will see what kind of people these are, dodging behind the bushes yonder," said he. As the Spaniards drew near shore they could see many fleeing figures.

"What a pity they are so afraid," said Cabrillo. "If we are to learn anything of the country, we must teach them that we mean them no harm."

"Master," said Pepe, "there are three of them hiding behind those bushes."

"Is it so, lad? Then go you up to them. They will not fear you." So the Indian boy walked slowly forward, holding out his hands with his palms upward, which not only let the natives see that he was unarmed, but in the sign language meant peace and friendship. As he drew near to them an old man and two younger ones, dressed in scanty shirts of rabbit-skins, came from their hiding places and began to talk to Pepe, but, though they also were Indians, they did not speak his language. Some of their words were evidently similar to his, and by these and the help of signs he partly understood what they said. Presently he returned to the group on shore.

"They say there are Spaniards back in the country a few days' journey from here."

"Spaniards? That is impossible," returned Cabrillo.

"They say that they are bearded, wear clothes like yours, and have white faces," answered the boy, simply.

"They must be mistaken, or perhaps you did not understand them fully," said the master. "At another time we will question them further. Now, give them this present of beads and hurry back, for it is late."

That night some of the men from the ships went on shore to fish. While they were drawing their nets, the Indians stole up softly and discharged their arrows, wounding three. The boy Juan had the most serious injury, an arrow being so deeply embedded in his shoulder that it could not be removed until they reached the ship. There the padre, who, like most priests of that day, knew something of surgery, drew it out, and bound up the shoulder in soothing balsams.

On the second day of their stay in port the wind began to blow from the southwest; the waves grew rough, and Cabrillo ordered the ships to be made ready for the tempest, which soon became violent. Meantime, Juan lay suffering in his hammock, which swung backward and forward with the motion of the ship. Suddenly he heard a step beside him and felt a cool hand on his forehead.

"How goes it, lad?" said Cabrillo, for it was the master himself. "You are suffering in a good cause. Have courage; you will soon be well. Remember, you have helped to discover a harbor, the like of which is seldom found. This storm is a severe one. I can hear the surf booming on the farther shore, yet our ship shows no strain on the anchor. Good harbor though it is, I am sorely disappointed, as I had hoped it was the entrance to the strait, the strait that seems a phantom flying before us as we go, drawing us onward to we know not what." The sadness of the captain's voice troubled Juan.

"Master," he asked earnestly, "what is the strait? I hear of it often, yet no one can tell me what it is, or where it lies."

"Because no one knows," answered the captain, rising. "I am needed on deck, but I will send old Tomas to tell you its strange story."

"The secret of the strait," said old Tomas, as he seated himself beside Juan, "has led many men to gallant deeds and also many a man to a gallant death. Always, since as a lad I first went to sea, the merchants of many lands have been seeking a safe and speedy way of reaching the Indies, where are found such foods, spices, and jewels as one sees nowhere else in the world.

"My father and grandfather used to travel with caravans overland to and from India. There are several routes, each controlled by some one of the great Italian cities, but all have somewhere to cross the desert, where the trains are often robbed by wild tribes. Sometimes, as they come nearer home, they are held by the Turks for heavy tribute, with such loss that the merchants have been forced to turn to the sea in hopes that a better way might be found. It was while searching for this route that Columbus discovered the new world, and when the news of his success was brought back to Europe there was great rejoicing, because it was thought that he had reached some part of India. Magellan's voyage, however, destroyed these hopes. He sailed for months down the eastern shore of the new land, and discovered, far away to the south, a strait through which he reached the great South Sea, but then he still sailed on for nearly a year before he came to the Spice Islands and Asia.

"Now every one believes that somewhere through this land to the north of us there is a wide, deep sea passage from the North Sea [Atlantic] to the South Sea [Pacific], by which ships may speedily reach India. This passage is called the Strait of Anian.

"The great captain, Hernando Cortez, the conqueror of New Spain [Mexico] spent many years and a large fortune seeking for this water way. Four different expeditions he sent out to explore this coast: most of them at his own cost. In the second one his pilot, Jiminez, led a mutiny, murdered his captain, and afterward discovered, accidentally, the southern point of this land we are now exploring. But it was not the good fortune of the noble Cortez to discover the strait. Our captain is the next to take up the search, and may God send him success."

After a stay of nearly a week in the bay of San Diego, Cabrillo continued his voyage up the coast, sailing by day, anchoring at night. He touched at an island which he named San Salvador, but which we know as Santa Catalina. Here, by his kind and generous treatment, he won the friendship of the natives. From this beautiful spot, he sailed, one Sunday morning, to the mainland. Entering the Bay of San Pedro, he found it enveloped in smoke.

"It seems a fair port," said the commander, "but go no farther inland. Drop anchor while we can see our way. We may well call this the Bay of Smokes." The fires, they found, had been started by the Indians to drive the rabbits from shelter, so they could be the more easily killed.

Sailing on, the ships anchored off a thickly settled valley, where the town of Ventura now lies. Here, on October 12, 1542, Cabrillo and his company went on shore and took solemn possession of the land in the name of the king of Spain and the viceroy of Mexico. Here, and along the channel, the people were better-looking, more comfortably lodged and clothed, than those farther south. They also had good canoes, which the natives of the lower coast did not possess. Pushing on, the explorer saw and noted the channel islands and rounded Point Conception. From here he was driven back by contrary winds, and toward nightfall of a stormy day found himself near the little island now named San Miguel.

"We will call it La Posesion and take it for our own," said Cabrillo, "for, if we can but make it, there seems to be a good harbor here." The storm, however, grew more severe. The sea rose until occasionally the waves swept over the smaller ship, which was without a deck. Here occurred a most unhappy accident. Something about the ship, a spar probably, loosened by the storm, fell and struck the brave commander, breaking his arm. Although severely injured, he would not have the wounds dressed until, after a long period of anxiety, the two ships entered in safety the little harbor of San Miguel.

Here, stormbound, they remained for a week. When they ventured forth, they again met with high winds and bad weather. Cabrillo, who in spite of discouragements never forgot his search for the strait, pushed close inshore and kept much of the time on deck looking for some signs of a river or passage. One morning at day-break, after a rough night, they found themselves drifting in an open bay.

"It is a fine roadstead," said Cabrillo, coming on deck, as the sun rose over the pine-covered hills. "Were it smaller, it would be a welcome harbor. We will name it from those majestic trees La Bahia de Pinos, and yonder long projection we will call the Cabo de Pinos." That bay is now called Monterey, but the cape still bears the name given it by this first explorer.

Anchoring in forty-five fathoms of water, they tried to go on shore, in order to take possession of the land, but the sea was so rough that they could not launch their boats. The next day they discovered and named some mountains which they called Sierra Nevada, and, sailing on, went as far north as about 401. But this winter voyage was made at a great sacrifice. The exposure and hardships, following the wound he had received, were too much for even the hardy sailor Juan Rodriguez Cabrillo. After weeks of struggle with storms, the ships were forced back to their old shelter at San Miguel. Here Christmas week was spent, but a sad holiday it was to the explorers, for their brave leader lay dying. Nobly had he done his duty up to the last.

"Juan," he said, to his young attendant, on Christmas Eve, "how gladly the bells will be ringing in Lisbon to-night. I seem to hear them now. They drive out all other sounds. Call Ferrelo and let no one else come but the padre." Very soon Juan returned with Cabrillo's first assistant, the pilot, Ferrelo, a brave navigator and a just man.

"Ferrelo," said Cabrillo, faintly, "Death calls me, and the duty I lay down you must take up. I command you to push the expedition northward at all hazards, and to keep such records as are necessary in order that fitting account of our voyage shall be given to the world. Will you promise me to do this?"

"I will, my master," said Ferrelo, simply. "To the best of my ability will I take up your work."

"Always looking for the strait, Ferrelo?"

"Always, senor."

On the 3d of January, 1543, the brave man died and was buried in the sands of Cuyler Harbor on San Miguel Island. His men called the island Juan Rodriguez. This name was afterwards dropped, but California should see to it that the island is rechristened in honor of the great sailor who sleeps there.

Ferrelo later succeeded in sailing as far north as Cape Mendocino and perhaps as far as 42i, but, though he kept as close to the shore as possible, he failed to discover the great bay whose waters, spreading like a sheet of silver over sixty miles of country, lay hidden just behind the Golden Gate. Near the Oregon line he was driven back by storms, and returned to Mexico, where he published a full account of the voyage.

Drake

In the town of Offenburg, Germany, there is a statue of a man standing on the deck of a ship, leaning against an anchor, his right hand grasping a map of America, his left, a cluster of bulbous roots. On the pedestal is the inscription, "Sir Francis Drake, the introducer of potatoes into Europe in the year of our Lord 1586."

While it is doubtful whether this honor really belongs to Drake, an Englishman, seeing the statue, would be inclined to say, "Is this all that Germany has to tell of the great captain who led our navy against the Spanish Armada; the first Englishman to sail around the world; the most daring explorer, clever naval commander, expert seaman, brave soldier, loyal friend, and gallant enemy of his time?" A Spaniard, on the contrary, might well exclaim, "Why did Germany erect a statue to this terrible man whom our poets call Dragontea [Dragon], this greatest of all pirates, this terror of the sea?" All this, and more, might be said of one man, who began life as a ship's boy.

At the time Drake first went to sea, England and Spain were by no means friendly. Henry the Eighth of England had ill-treated his wife, who was a Spanish princess. In addition he had drawn the English people away from the Church of Rome. These things were most displeasing to Spain, but there was still another reason for disagreement. The interests of the two countries were opposed commercially, and this was the most important cause of contention.

Spain claimed by right of discovery, and gift of the Pope of Rome, all the land in the new world except Brazil (which belonged to Portugal), and held that no explorers or tradesmen, other than her own, had any rights on her waters or in her ports. English seamen denied much of this claim, and so frequent were the disputes arising upon the subject that the English sailors adopted as a maxim, "No peace beyond the line," meaning the line which was, by the Pope's decree, the eastern boundary of the Spanish claim.

The favorite prey of the British mariners was the treasure ships carrying to Spain the precious cargoes of gold and silver from the rich mines of the new world. With the far richer ships of the Philippine and Indian trade, sailing on unknown waters, they had not, up to Drake's time, been able to interfere.

Drake, when a very young man, had joined a trading expedition to Mexico. While there the English were attacked by the Spanish in what the former considered a most treacherous manner. Drake's brother and many of his comrades were killed, and their goods taken. After the battle he solemnly vowed to be revenged, and so thoroughly did he carry out his resolution that he was for years the terror of the Spanish seamen, and, by many of the superstitious common sailors, believed to be Satan himself come to earth in human form.

Shortly after this unfortunate expedition Drake engaged in a marauding voyage to Panama, where he captured rich stores of gold and silver and precious stones. He gained such renown for his bravery and seamanship that upon coming home he found himself famous.

Queen Elizabeth knew that Spain was opposed to her and her religion, and was not in her heart displeased when her brave seamen got the better of their Spanish rivals. She received Drake privately, and help was offered him secretly from people who stood high in the government. With this encouragement he resolved to embark on a most hazardous and daring adventure. While in Panama he had seen, from a "high and goodlie tree" on a mountain side, the great Pacific, and was immediately filled with a desire to sail on its waters and explore its shores. He therefore determined to cross the Atlantic, pass through the Strait of Magellan, up the Pacific, and to plunder the Spanish towns along the coast of South and Central America, until he should reach the region traversed by the richly laden Spanish ships coming from India and the Philippines. It is said that the queen herself put a thousand crowns into this venture. One thing is certain, that he received sufficient help to fit out five small vessels, with one hundred and sixty-four men. With these he sailed from Falmouth, England, in December of 1577. With the exception of perhaps one or two of the rich men who had helped him, no one, not even his men, knew of his plans.

After a long and interesting voyage in which one vessel was lost and the others, though he did not know it, had deserted him, he found himself with but one ship beating his way up the coast of Lower California. This was his flagship Pelican, which he had rechristened the Golden Hind. It was then so laden with rich booty, that it was like a hawk which had stolen too heavy a chicken, driven this way and that by the winds, scarcely able to reach its nest.

In addition to a good store of Chile wines and foods of various kinds, there were packed away in the hold of the Golden Hind, twenty-five thousand pesos of gold, eight thousand pounds of English money, and a great cross of gold with "emeralds near as large as a man's finger." From one vessel Drake had taken one hundred-weight of silver; from a messenger of the mines, who was sleeping beside a spring on the Peruvian coast, thirteen bars of solid silver; off the backs of a train of little gray llamas, the camels of the Andes, eight hundred pounds of silver; and besides all these were large quantities of gold and silver that were not recorded in the ship's list, and stores of pearls, diamonds, emeralds, silks, and porcelain.

The last prize taken was the Spanish treasure ship Cacafuegos. Drake had transferred its cargo and crew to his own vessel and, for a time, manned it with some of his men. Its noble commander, St. John de Anton, who had been wounded in the attack, received every possible attention on the English vessel, and in the report which he afterwards made to the viceroy of Mexico, he told of the perfect order and discipline maintained on the Golden Hind, and of the luxury which surrounded its commander, who was treated with great reverence by his men.

Before sailing on to the northward, Drake restored St. John and his crew to their vessel. Then, because he feared that they might fall into the hands of his fleet (having no suspicion that the other captains had returned home), he gave the Spaniards the following letter, which shows the great Englishman to have been more honorable than he is oftentimes represented:--

"To Master Weinter and the Masters of the Other Ships of my Fleet:

"If it pleaseth God that you should chance to meet with this ship of St. John de Anton, I pray you use him well according to my promise given him. If you want to use anything that is in the ship, I pray you pay him double value for it, which I will satisfy again. And command your men not to do any harm and what agreement we have made, at my return unto England, I will, by God's help, perform, although I am in doubt that this letter will ever come to your hand, notwithstanding I am the man I have promised to be.

"Beseeching God, the Saviour of the world, to have us all in his keeping, to whom I give all honor, praise, and glory,

"Your sorrowful captain, whose heart is heavy for you,

"Francis Drake."

How to get home was the problem which this daring man had now to solve. There was no possibility of returning by the way he had come. He well knew that the news of his departure had reached Spain, and that her war ships would be waiting for him, not only at the eastern entrance of the Strait of Magellan, but at the Isthmus and in the Caribbean Sea.

If by sailing northward he could find the Strait of Anian, then his homeward journey would be safe and short; but if he could not find that illusive body of water, then there was left to him but the Pacific for a highway. However, this did not daunt him, as he felt that what the Portuguese Magellan had done, Drake the Englishman could do.

Keeping well out from shore, the Golden Hind now sailed northward for nearly two months. Drake passed just west of the Farallon Islands, never dreaming of the great harbor which lay so short a distance on the other side. He traveled as far north as latitude 42i or possibly 43i, and perhaps he even landed at one point, but he failed to find the strait. According to Fletcher, the priest of the Church of England who kept a journal of the expedition, they were finally forced by the extreme cold to turn southward. "Here," says Fletcher, "it pleased God on this 17th day of June, 1579, to send us, in latitude 38i, a convenient fit harbor." This is now supposed to be Drakes Bay, which lies thirty miles northwest of San Francisco, in Marin county.

"In this bay we anchored, and the people of the country having their houses close to the waterside showed themselves unto us and sent presents to our general. He, in return, courteously treated them and liberally bestowed upon them things necessary to cover their nakedness.

"Their houses are digged around about with earth and have for the brim of that circle, clefts of wood set upon the ground and joined closely together at the top like the spire of a steeple, which by reason of this closeness are very warm. The men go naked, but the women make themselves loose garments knit about the middle, while over their shoulders they wear the skin of a deer."

These people brought presents and seemed to want to offer sacrifices to the strangers as gods, but Drake, hastily calling his men together, held divine services, "To which, especially the prayers and music," says Fletcher, "they were most attentive and seemed to be greatly affected." The Bible used by Drake in this service is still to be seen in Nut Hall House, Devonshire, England.

Presently a messenger came, saying that the king wished to visit them if they would assure him of their peaceful intentions. Drake sent him presents, then marched his force into a kind of fort he had had made in which to place such parts of the cargo as it was necessary to remove in order to careen the ship for repairing. The coming of the chief is thus described:--

"He came in princely majesty. In the fore-front was a man of goodly personage who bore the scepter whereon was hung two crowns with chains of marvelous length. The crowns were made of knit-work wrought with feathers of divers colors, the chains being made of bony substances.

"Next came the king with his guard, all well clothed in connie skins, then the naked common people with faces painted, each bearing some presents. After ceremonies consisting of speeches and dances, they offered one of the crowns to Drake, who, accepting in the name of Elizabeth, allowed it to be placed on his head."

While the men were busy cleaning and repairing the ship, the commander and his officers made excursions into the interior, visiting many Indian towns and passing through wide plains where vast herds of deer, often one thousand or more, all large and fat, were feeding on the rich grasses. They also saw great numbers of what they called connies, which, from their description, must have been ground squirrels, or else some variety of animal now extinct. The country Drake named New Albion, partly from its white cliffs, which resembled those of his native land, and partly in belief that it would be easier to lay claim to the country if it bore one of the names applied to England.

"When the time came for our departure," continued Fletcher in his journal, "our general set up a monument of our being here, so also, of her majesty's right and title to the land: namely a plate nailed upon a fair great post, whereon was engraved her majesty's name, the day and year of our arrival, with the giving up of the province and people into her majesty's hands, together with her highness' picture and arms in a sixpence under the plate, whereunder was also written the name of our general."

Fletcher seemed not to know of Cabrillo's voyage, for he claimed that no one had ever discovered land in this region, or for many degrees to the south; while in fact Ferrelo with Cabrillo's ships had sailed as far north as latitude 42i, although we have no reason to think that he landed in a higher latitude than that of Point Conception and San Miguel Island.

Once again solemn religious services were held by the Englishmen on the hospitable soil that had been their home for over a month. Then they went on board the ship, accompanied to the shore by the grieving Indians, who would not be comforted when they saw their new friends forsaking them. It was near the last of July in 1579 that Captain Drake with his brave men began his wonderful homeward voyage.

It was a triumphant return they made in September, a year later. Crowds flocked to see the famous ship and its gallant commander.

Some of the queen's statesmen strongly disapproved of Drake's attack upon Spanish towns and vessels, and felt he should be arrested and tried for piracy; but the common people cheered him wherever he went, and as a crowning honor, in the luxurious cabin of his good ship Golden Hind, he was visited by the great Elizabeth herself. When the banquet was over, at the queen's command, he bent his knee before her, and this sovereign, who, though a woman, dearly loved such courage and daring as he had displayed, tapped him on the shoulder and bade him arise "Sir Francis Drake."

Galli and Carmenon

In 1584 Francisco Galli, commanding a Philippine ship, returning to Mexico by way of Japan, sighted the coast of California in latitude 37i 30'. He saw, as he reported, "a high and fair land with no snow and many trees, and in the sea, drifts of roots, reeds, and leaves." Some of the latter he gathered and cooked with meat for his men, who were no doubt suffering from scurvy.

Galli wrote of the point where he first saw the coast as Cape Mendocino, which would seem to imply that the point had been discovered and named at some previous time, of which, however, there is no record.

In 1595 Sebastian Carmenon, commanding the ship San Agustin, coming from the Philippines, was given royal orders to make some explorations on the coast of

California, probably to find a suitable harbor for Manila vessels. In doing so he was so unfortunate as to run his vessel ashore behind Point Reyes, and to lighten her was obliged to leave behind a portion of his cargo, consisting of wax and silks in boxes. There is only the briefest record of this voyage, and no report of any discoveries.

Vizcaino

Almost sixty years after the voyage of Cabrillo, came a royal order from the king of Spain to the viceroy of Mexico which, translated from the Spanish, ran something like this:--

"Go, search the northern coast of the Californias, until you find a good and sufficient harbor wherein my Manila galleons may anchor safe and protected, and where may be founded a town that my scurvy-stricken sailors may find the fresh food necessary for their relief. Furthermore, spare no expense."

The destruction of Spanish shipping by Drake and other English seamen who followed his example, had caused great anxiety to the Spaniards and was partly the reason for this order.

"Send for Don Sebastian," said the viceroy. "He is a brave gentleman and good sailor. He shall carry out the order of the king." But it took time to fit out such an expedition, and it was not until an afternoon in May, 1602, that Don Sebastian Vizcaino, on his flagship, the San Diego, sailed out of the harbor of Acapulco into the broad Pacific. Closely following him were his other ships, the San Thomas and Tres Reyes.

There had been solemn services at the cathedral that afternoon. Officers and men had taken of the holy communion; and now their wives and children stood on the island at the entrance of the harbor, watching the white sails as they grew fainter and fainter and at last disappeared in the haze of the coming night.

Then the watchers returned to their lonely homes with heavy hearts, for in those days few came back who sailed out on the great South Sea. Storms, battles with the natives, and scurvy made sad havoc among the sailors.

Early in November Vizcaino entered "a famous port," which he named San Diego, finding it, as Padre Ascension's journal says, "beautiful and very grand, and all parts of it very convenient shelter from the winds." After leaving San Diego, the next anchoring place was the island named by Vizcaino for Santa Catalina, on whose feast day his ships entered the pretty little harbor of Avalon.

The Spaniards were greatly pleased with the island and also with the people, whom they described as being a large-figured, light-complexioned race; all, men, women, and children, being well clothed in sealskins. They had large dwellings, many towns, and fine canoes. What struck Padre Ascension most strongly was their temple, of which he says: "There was in the temple a large level court, and about this a circle surrounded by feather work of different colors taken from various birds which I understand had been sacrificed to their idols. Within this circle was the figure of a demon painted in color after the manner of the Indians of New Spain. On its sides were figures of the sun and moon.

"It so fell out that when our soldiers came up from the ships to view the temple, there were in the circle two immense ravens, far larger than ordinary. When the men arrived, they flew away to some rocks that were near by, and the soldiers seeing how large they were, raised their arquebuses and killed them both. Then did the Indians begin to weep and make great lamentation. I understand that the devil was accustomed to speak to them, through these birds, for which they showed great respect."

There were in the island quantities of edible roots of a variety of the yucca called gicamas, and many little bulbs which the Spanish called "papas pequenos" (little potatoes). These, the padre said, the Indians took in their canoes over to the mainland, thus making their living by barter. This certainly must have been the beginning of commerce on the coast.

Vizcaino entered and named the Bay of San Pedro. To the channel islands he also gave the names which they now bear. Sailing on, he discovered a river which he named "Carmelo," in honor of the Carmelite friars who accompanied him. The same day the fleet rounded the long cape called "Point Pinos" and came to anchor in the bay formed by its projection. From here the San Tomas was sent to Mexico to carry the sick, of whom there were many, and to bring back fresh supplies. The men who remained were at once set to work. Some supplied the two ships with wood and water; others built a chapel of brush near the beach, under a large oak at the roots of which flowed a spring of delicious water. In this chapel mass was said and the Te Deum chanted. For over one hundred and fifty years this oak was known, both in New Spain and at the court of the king, as the "Oak of Vizcaino, in the Bay of Monterey." From here Vizcaino wrote to the king of Spain as follows:--

"Among the ports of greater consideration which I have discovered is one in 30i north latitude which I called Monterey, as I wrote to your majesty in December. It is all that can be desired for commodiousness and as a station for ships making the voyage from the Philippines, sailing whence they make a landfall on this coast. It is sheltered from all winds and in the immediate vicinity are pines from which masts of any desired size could be obtained, as well as live oak, white oak, and other woods. There is a variety of game, great and small. The land has a genial climate and the waters are good. It is thickly settled by a people whom I find to be of gentle disposition, and whom I believe can be brought within the fold of the Holy Gospel and subjugation to your majesty."

This enthusiastic praise of the harbor of Monterey by a man who was familiar with the port of San Diego, caused much trouble later, as will be seen in the study of the founding of the missions.

Not waiting for the return of the San Tomas, Vizcaino with his two ships soon sailed northward, and reached a point in about latitude 42i, which was probably the northern limit reached by Cabrillo's ships and only a little lower than the farthest explorations of Drake. Although Vizcaino was looking for harbors, he yet passed twice outside the Bay of San Francisco, the finest on the coast, without discovering it. After his return to Mexico, Vizcaino endeavored to raise an expedition to found a settlement at Monterey, even going to Spain to press the matter; but other schemes were demanding the king's attention, and he would give neither thought nor money to affairs in the new world; and so, thoroughly disheartened Vizcaino returned to Mexico.

From this time for over one hundred and fifty years there is no record of explorations along this coast, either by vessels from Mexico or by those coming from the Philippines. California seemed again forgotten.

This is the story of the few voyages made to the coast of California previous to its settlement. The first, under Cabrillo, was sent out by the viceroy Mendoza, who hoped to gain fame and riches by the discovery of the Strait of Anian, and by finding wealthy countries and cities which were supposed to exist in the great northwest, about which much was imagined but nothing known.

Drake planned his voyage largely in pursuit of his revenge upon Spain, partly for the plunder which he hoped to obtain from the Spanish towns and vessels along the Pacific coast of America, and partly because of his desire to explore the Pacific Ocean.

Vizcaino also was expected to search for the strait, but he was especially sent out to find a good harbor and place for settlement on the California coast. This was intended in a great measure for the benefit of the Philippine trade, but also to aid in holding the country for Spain.

Chapter IV
The Cross of Santa Fe

The kings highway which led up from Vera Cruz, the chief port of the eastern coast of Mexico, to the capital city of New Spain had in the eighteenth century more history connected with it than any other road in the new world. Over it had passed Montezuma with all the splendor of his pagan court. On it, too, had marched and counter marched his grim conqueror, the great Cortez. Through its white dust had traveled an almost endless procession of mules and slaves, carrying the treasures of the mines of Mexico and the rich imports of Manila and India on toward Spain.

Over this road there was journeying, one winter day in the year 1749, a traveler of more importance to the history of the state of California than any one who had gone before. He was no great soldier or king, only a priest in the brownish gray cloak of the order of St. Francis. He was slight in figure, and limped painfully from a sore on his leg, caused, it is supposed, by the bite of some poisonous reptile. The chance companions who traveled with him begged him to stop and rest beside a stream, but he would not. Then, as he grew more weary, they entreated him to seek shelter in a ranch house near by and give up his journey.

"Speak not to me thus. I am determined to continue. I seem to hear voices of unconverted thousands calling me," was all the answer he gave. So on foot, with no luggage but his prayer book, he limped out of sight --the humble Spanish priest, Junipero Serra.

While only a schoolboy, young Serra had been more interested in the Indian inhabitants of the new world than in boyish pleasure. As he grew older it became his greatest desire to go to them as a missionary. At eighteen he became a priest;

but it was not until his thirty-sixth year that he gained the opportunity of which he had so long dreamed, when, in company with a body of missionaries, among whom were his boyhood friends, Francisco Palou and Juan Crespi, he landed at Vera Cruz.

He was too impatient to begin his new work, to wait for the government escort which was coming to meet them. So he started out on foot, with only such companions as he might pick up by the way, to make the long journey to the city of Mexico.

Sixteen years later, attended by a gay company of gentlemen and ladies, there traveled over this road one of Spain's wisest statesmen, Jose de Galvez, whom the king had sent out to look after affairs in the new world. Flourishing settlements were by this time scattered over a large portion of Mexico, and even in the peninsula of Lower California there were a number of missions. It was almost a hundred years before this time that two Catholic priests of the Society of Jesus had asked permission to found mission settlements among the Indians of this peninsula.

"You may found the missions if you like, but do not look to us for money to help you," was the answer returned by the officers of the government. So the two Jesuit priests set about collecting funds for the work.

They were eloquent men, and the people who heard them preach became so interested in the Indians that they were glad to give. And so, little by little, this fund grew. As the good work went on, greater gifts poured in. Whole fortunes were left them, and finally they had a very large sum carefully invested in the city of Mexico. This was known as the Pius Fund. From it was taken all the money needed for the founding of the missions of Lower California; and, many years later, the expenses of founding the twenty-one missions of Upper California came from the same source. This fund became the subject of a long dispute between Mexico and the United States, of which an account is given in Chapter XI.

In 1767 all the Jesuit priests in New Spain were called back to Europe, and a large portion of their wealth and missions on the peninsula were given over to the order of St. Francis, with Junipero Serra at their head. It was Galvez's duty to superintend this change, and while he was on his way to the peninsula for that purpose he was overtaken by an order from the king of Spain to occupy and fortify the ports of San Diego and Monterey. The Spanish government had the description of these ports furnished by Vizcaino in his account of his explorations in Upper and Lower California over one hundred and sixty years before.

The articles of the king's order were: first, to establish the Catholic faith; second, to extend Spanish dominion; third, to check the ambitious schemes of a foreign power; and lastly, to carry out a plan formed by Philip the Third, as long ago as 1603, for the establishment of a town on the California coast where there was a harbor suitable for ships of the Manila trade.

Galvez at once proceeded to organize four expeditions for the settlement of Upper California, two by land, two by sea. Captain Portola, governor of the peninsula, was put in command, with good leaders under him. Still, Galvez was not satisfied.

"This is all very well," he said; "these men will obey my orders, but they do not care much whether this land is settled or not, and if discouragements arise, back they will come, and I shall have the whole thing to do over again. I must find some one who is interested in the work, some one who will not find anything impossible. I think I shall send for that lame, pale-faced priest, with the beautiful eyes, who has taken up the work of these missions so eagerly."

"So you think we can make the venture a success?" asked Galvez, after he had talked over his plans with Junipero.

"Surely," said Padre Serra, his eyes shining, his whole face glowing with enthusiasm. "It is God's work to carry the cross of the holy faith [Santa Fe] into the wilderness, and He will go with us; can you not hear the heathen calling us to bring them the blessed Gospel? I can see that I have lived all my life for this glorious day."

Then they went to work, the priest and the king's counselor--down on the wharf, even working with their own hands, packing away the cargo.

"Hurry! Hurry!" said Galvez. The word was passed along, and in a short time the four expeditions were ready.

Many were the trials and discouragements of the various parties. Scurvy was so severe among the sailors that one ship lost all its crew save two men, and there were a number of deaths on another ship; while a third vessel which started later was never heard from. Padre Junipero, who accompanied the second land party, under the charge of Governor Portola, became so ill from the wound on his leg that the commander urged him to return; but he would not. Calling a muleteer who was busy after the day's march, doctoring the sores on his animals, he said:--

"Come, my son, and cure my sores also."

"Padre," exclaimed the man, shocked at the idea, "I am no surgeon; I doctor only my beasts."

"Think then that I am a beast, my child," said the padre, "and treat me accordingly."

The man obeyed. Gathering some leaves of the malva, or cheese plant, he bruised them a little, heated them on the stones of the camp fire, and spreading them with warm tallow, applied them to the wound. The next morning the leg was so much better that the cure was thought to be a miracle. Still the padre was very weak; and there was great rejoicing in the party when at last they looked down from a height on San Diego Bay, with the two ships--the San Carlos and the San Antonio--riding at anchor, white tents on the beach, and soldiers grouped about. Salutes were fired by the newcomers and returned by the soldiers and ships, and very soon the four expeditions were reunited.

On the next day, Sunday, solemn thanksgiving services were held. Then for fourteen days all were busy attending to the sick, making ready for the departure of the ship San Antonio, which was to be sent back for supplies, and packing up food and other necessities for the journey to Monterey. The San Antonio sailed on the 9th of July, 1769, and five days later Governor Portola and two thirds of the well portion of the company started overland to Monterey.

Meantime Padre Junipero had been impatiently awaiting an opportunity to begin his great work--the conversion of the heathen. He had written back in his own peculiar way to his friend Padre Palou, whom he left in charge of the missions of Lower California.

"Long Live Jesus, Joseph, and Mary, This to Fray Francisco Palou.

"My dear friend and Sir:--

"I, thanks be to God, arrived day before yesterday at this, in truth, beautiful, and with reason famous, port of San Diego. We find Gentiles [the name given to the wild Indians] here in great numbers. They seem to lead temperate lives on various seeds and on fish which they catch from their rafts of tule which are formed like a canoe."

The second day after the departure of Portola and his party, Sunday, July 16,

Padre Serra felt that the glorious moment for which he had so long prayed had at length arrived. The mission bells were unpacked and hung on a tree, and a neophyte, or converted Indian, whom he had brought with him from the peninsula, was appointed to ring them. As the sweet tones sounded on the clear air, all the party who were able gathered about the padre, who stood lifting the cross of Christ on high. All joined in solemnly chanting a hymn, and a sermon was preached. Then with more chanting, the tolling of, the bells, and the firing of muskets, was concluded the ceremony of the founding of the first of the California missions, that of San Diego.

Portola and his men, in spite of many discouragements, traveled steadily northward for nearly two months until at last, one October morning, they saw what they thought to be Point Pinos, the name given by Cabrillo to the pine-covered cape to the south of Monterey Bay. They were right in thinking this Point Pinos, but the sad part is that when they climbed a hill and looked down on the bay they had come so far to find, they failed to recognize it.

They tramped wearily over the sun-dried hills that bordered it, and walked on its sandy beach, but could not believe the wide, open roadstead, encircled by bare brown heights, could be the well-inclosed port lying at the foot of hills richly green, so warmly described by Vizcaino in his winter voyage. It was a great disappointment, for this was the latitude in which they had expected to find Monterey. After talking it over, they decided they must be still too far south, so they tramped on for many days.

On the last day of October, those of the party who were well enough, climbed a high hill--(Point San Pedro on the west coast of the peninsula)--and were rewarded by a glorious view. On their left the great ocean stretched away to the horizon line, its waves breaking in high-tossed foam on the rocky shore beneath them. Before them they saw an open bay, or roadstead, lying between the point on which they stood, and one extending into the sea far to the northwest. Upon looking at their map of Vizcaino's voyage, they rightly decided that this farther projection was Point Reyes; the little bay sheltered by the curve of its arm was the one named on the map St. Francis, and now known as Drakes Bay. Well out to sea they discovered a group of rocky islands which they called Farallones; but not a man who stood on the height dreamed that only a short distance to the right up the rocky coast there lay a bay so immense and so perfectly inclosed that it would ever be one of the wonders of the land they were exploring.

On account of the sick of the party, among whom were the commander and his lieutenant, it was decided to travel no further, but to camp here while Sergeant Ortega was dispatched to follow the coast line to Point Reyes and explore the little bay it inclosed.

With a few men and three days' provisions consisting of small cakes made of bran and water, which was the only food they had left, this brave Spanish officer marched away, little imagining the honor which was soon to be his. Leading this expedition, he was the first white man to explore the peninsula where now stands the guardian city of the western coast, and we must wonder what were his thoughts when, pushing his way up some brush-covered heights, he came out suddenly upon the great bay we call San Francisco.

What a mighty surprise was that sixty miles of peaceful water that had so long remained hidden from European explorers, baffling the anxious gaze of Cabrillo, the faithful explorations of Ferrelo, the eagle eyes of Drake, and the earnest search of Vizcaino!

Pushing steadily on toward Point Reyes, Ortega encountered a second surprise, when from the Presidio hills he looked down on beautiful Golden Gate, whose rumpled waters seemed to say:--

"No farther can you come. We keep guard here."

Seeing that it was quite impossible for him to reach Point Reyes, Ortega decided to return to Portola. He found the commander and his party so weakened by sickness and the lack of food that it had been decided to explore no farther, but to return at once to the southern mission. After a painful march of sixty days the party reached San Diego.

Bitter was the disappointment of Padre Junipero Serra at the failure to found the mission of Monterey. he did not believe, as many of the party reported, that the bay was filled up with sand. Keener still was his grief when Portola, after looking over the supply of food, announced that unless the ship San Antonio or the sloop San Jose arrived by a certain date with provisions, they would have to abandon Upper California and return to the peninsula.

The padre at once called the people together for a nine days' session of prayer and other church services at which to pray for the coming of the relief boat. Portola, though he attended the services, went steadily on with his preparations for departure. On the morning of the day before the one set for the beginning of the march toward Lower California, the padres went to the heights overlooking the bay, where they remained watching and praying. At sea a heavy fog hung over the water. Hour after hour passed as they gazed out on the lovely bay. Noon came, but they would not return to the mission to rest or eat. The afternoon wore away, the sun sank in the clouds above the horizon, then, as all hope seemed gone, the fog was lifted by a sunset breeze, and there, far out at sea, they saw a white sail. The good men fell on their knees in thanksgiving, while their Indian servants ran to carry the news to camp.

This vessel, the San Antonio, brought not only abundant provisions but fresh orders from Galvez to hurry the work at Monterey. The settlement of Upper California was now made certain.

An expedition by land and the San Antonio by sea immediately started northward. A few weeks later Padre Junipero wrote to Padre Palou: "By the favor of God, after a month and a half of painful navigation, the San Antonio found anchor in this port of Monterey, which we find unvarying in circumstances and substance as described by Don Sebastian Vizcaino."

They even found Vizcaino's oak. Indeed, it is said on good authority, that the oak remained standing until 1838, when the high tides washed the earth from its roots so that it fell.

Soon the land expedition arrived, and one June morning in 1770 the members of the two parties, all in their best attire, were gathered on the beach for the purpose of founding the second mission. It must have been a pretty scene,--the stanch little vessel San Antonio, gay with bunting, swinging at anchor a short distance out, while on shore were grouped the sailors in the bright dress of seamen of those times, the soldiers in leather uniform, the governor and his staff in the handsome costumes of Spanish officials, and the padres in their gray robes. Close beside the oak a brush house had been built, bells hung, and an altar erected. While the bells tolled, the solemn service of dedication was held by Padre Junipero, and so was founded the Mission San Carlos de Borromeo at Monterey.

Near each of the earlier coast missions there was also founded a military station called a presidio, a name borrowed from the Roman presidium. The word meant a fort or fortified town. These presidios were intended to guard the safety of the missions from the wild Indians, and to defend the coast from ships of other countries.

After the religious services Governor Portola proceeded to found the presidio and take formal possession in the name of the king of Spain by hoisting and saluting the royal banner, pulling up bunches of grass, and casting stones, which was an ancient manner of taking possession of a piece of land or country. The presidio of Monterey was for a long time the site of the capital of Upper California and therefore most important in the history of the state.

For the sake of better land and water the mission site was soon removed about six miles, to the Carmelo River. Although not so wealthy as some of the missions, it was the home of Padre Junipero Serra, president of all the missions, and so its history is especially interesting.

The news of the settlement of San Diego and Monterey was received in Mexico with great joy, and it was resolved to found five more missions above San Diego. Four of these were San Gabriel, near the present site of Los Angeles; San Luis Obispo, farther north; San Antonio; and San Francisco. Before leaving the peninsula, Padre Serra had asked Galvez, "And for Father Francisco, head of our order, is there to be no mission for him?" To which Galvez had replied, "If Saint Francis wants a mission, let him cause his port to be found and it will be placed there." When the beautiful bay was discovered by Sergeant Ortega, it was thought that this might be the harbor Saint Francis intended for himself, but before naming it for the head of the order it was necessary that it should be explored. Although two land expeditions were sent up for this purpose, they were unsuccessful; and it was not until August, 1775, about four months after the eventful battle of Lexington had taken place on the Atlantic coast, that white men first entered the Bay of San Francisco in a ship.

Lieutenant Ayala of the Spanish navy, with the San Carlos, had the honor of conducting this expedition.

He reached the entrance to the bay just as night was coming on. Not liking to trust his vessel in a strange harbor, he sent forward a boat to make explorations, and then, as it was a little slow in returning, he daringly pushed on in the darkness into the unknown water. His small craft bobbed and plunged in the rough water of the bar, darted through Golden Gate, and came safely to anchor near North Beach.

Soon after this exploration it was settled that here Saint Francis should have his mission.

Padre Junipero Serra appointed his friend Francisco Palou, who had now joined him in his work in Upper California, to make this settlement, and on the 9th of October, 1776, there was founded in that portion of San Francisco known as the Mission District, at the corner of Sixteenth and Dolores streets, the mission of San Francisco. This is often called Mission Dolores from the name of a small lake and stream beside which it was built. To-day the name San Francisco rests not only on the old mission building, with its white pillars, but on the beautiful city which is the metropolis of our western coast.

As fast as possible Padre Junipero hastened the establishment of missions, choosing those places where there were the largest native settlements. In the vicinity of Monterey Bay there were, besides the San Carlos mission, Santa Cruz on the northern curve of the bay, and in the fertile valley back of the Santa Cruz Mountains the missions of Santa Clara, San Jose, and San Juan Bautista. Farther south on a lonely height stood Soledad, and much farther south, San Miguel.

The Indians along the Santa Barbara Channel, of whom there were a great many, were more intelligent and industrious than in other portions of the country settled by the missionaries, and here were the missions of Santa Barbara, San Buenaventura, La Purisima, and Santa Inez.

In the south, in the fertile valley where are now the great grain fields of Los Angeles county, San Fernando was founded. Between San Gabriel and San Diego were placed San Juan Capistrano, San Luis Rey, and the chapel of Pala. San Rafael and Solano, to the north of San Francisco Bay, complete the list of twenty-one missions of Upper California.

It is impossible to give more than the names of most of these missions, although about each many true and beautiful stories might be told. It would be well if those who live near one of these noble ruins would seek out its particular history and the stories connected with it. This would be interesting and helpful work for the students in the schools of the state.

The story of the missions seems like a fairy tale, wonderful and unreal. Into a wilderness inhabited only by savage men and wild animals, hundreds of miles from any civilized settlement, there came these men trained as simple priests.

Two by two they came, bringing with them, for the starting of each mission, a few soldiers, seven to ten, a few converted Indians from the missions of Lower California, a little live stock, some church furniture, and always the bells; yet in a little over forty years they had succeeded in founding a chain of missions whose sweet-toned bells chimed the hours and called to prayer from San Diego to the Bay of San Francisco.

Churches were built larger and often of a purer type of architecture than those in the civilized well-settled portions of the land,-- buildings that have lasted for a hundred years and may last many years longer if care is taken to preserve them. Canals of stone and cement and dams of masonry were constructed that would do credit to our best workmen of to-day.

The little packages of wheat and other grains, seeds from Spanish oranges and olives, little dried bundles of grapevines from Mexico, developed, under their care, into the great fields of grain, groves of oranges and olives, and the wide-spreading vineyards of the mission ranches. All these wonders were performed with Indian workmen trained by the padres.

But what the missionaries cared for more than their success in building and planting were the thousands of baptized Indians at each mission. These they instructed daily for the good of their souls in the truths of the Christian religion, while for their bodily needs they were taught to plow the earth, to plant seed, to raise and care for domestic animals. They learned also many useful trades; and music, frescoing, and art were taught those who seemed to have an especial taste for such things.

At the head of this great work was gentle Padre Junipero Serra, the most interesting character in the history of the missions. He was frail and slender and much worn by constant labor of head and hands, but his every thought and action seemed to be for others. Back and forth from Monterey to San Diego, from mission to mission, he traveled almost constantly, teaching, baptizing, confirming thousands of his dusky charges. He was president of all the missions, and besides this was bishop, doctor, judge, and architect, as well as steward of the mission products and money.

Associated with him in his work were a group of noble men whose lives were spent in caring for the native people with whom they worked and among whom they finally died. The inhabitants of California may well honor the mission padres for their earnest, unselfish lives, and in no way can this be done so fully as in the preservation of the grand old buildings they left behind, which are indeed fitting monuments to their devotion, energy, and skill.

Beginning with San Diego, let us, in fancy, visit the missions in the early part of the nineteenth century.

It is a winter day in the year 1813 when we ride up the broad, wind-swept road which leads to the newly dedicated mission building of San Diego. The wide plain that surrounds it is green with native grass and the blades of young wheat. Of the two hundred cattle, one hundred sheep, one hundred horses, and twenty asses brought up by Padre Junipero in 1769 to be divided among the earlier missions, San Diego had only its due share; yet under the wise management of the padres, they have now at this mission, feeding on the green plains, thousands of cattle, horses, and sheep, which are tended by comfortably clothed Indian herders. Near the mission are the green and gold of orange orchards, the gray of the olive, and the bare branches of extensive vineyards. At one side we see a large kitchen garden where young Indians are at work planting and hoeing.

As we draw up in front of the church, Indian servants come out to take our horses. We dismount, and a padre who is superintending work in the orchard comes and welcomes us with gentle courtesy. He sends us a servant to show us to our room, a small square apartment with a hard earthen floor and bare, whitewashed walls with no ornament but a cross. The beds are of rawhide stretched over a frame. The covering consists of sheets of coarse cotton grown and woven at the southern missions, and blankets, coarse but warm, made by the Indians from the wool of the mission sheep.

Dinner at the padre's table we find most enjoyable. There is beef and chicken, the frijole, or red bean of Spain, and other vegetables prepared in a tasty manner peculiar to Spanish cooking, so we do not doubt that the cook has been taught his trade by the padre himself. The Indian boys who wait on the table also show careful training, performing their duties quickly and quietly. Here we can find for bread the tortilla,--still the food of the Indian and Mexican people of California. It is a thin cake made of meal or flour and water, and baked without grease on a hot stone or griddle. Wines made at the mission, the favorite chocolate, thick and sweet, and some fruit from the padre's garden complete the meal.

Dinner over, we visit the church and admire the striking contrast between the red tiles of the roof and the creamy white of the walls. All the buildings are made of bricks molded from a clay called adobe and dried slowly in the sun. Each brick is twelve inches square by four inches thick, and the walls are laid two or three bricks deep, those of the church itself being nearly four feet in thickness. It seems almost impossible that so large and well made a building could have been constructed by untrained workmen. Next to the church are the rooms of the padres, then the dining room and the quarters of the mission guard, which consists apparently of but two men, the rest being at the presidio, several miles away. Adjoining these are the storehouses and shops of the Indian workmen, all of which open on the great courtyard.

In the courtyard is a busy scene. Blacksmiths with hammer and anvil make sounding blows as they work up old iron into needed farm utensils. The soap maker's caldron sends up a cloud of ill-smelling steam. At one side carpenters are at work trimming and cutting square holes in logs for the beams of new buildings which the padres wish to put up. Saddle makers, squatted on the ground, are busy fashioning saddletrees, carving, and sewing leather. The shoemaker is hard at work with needle and awl. These and many other trades are all going on at once. These courts, which are called patios, were generally several acres in extent and at the most flourishing period of the missions each settlement often gave shelter to over a thousand people.

Behind the central court is the home of the unmarried women. This, and the rooms for their work, open on a separate square where there is shade from orange and fig trees and a bathing pond supplied by the zanja, or water ditch. Here square-figured, heavy-featured Indian girls are busy spinning and weaving thread into cloth. Others are cutting out and sewing garments. Some, squatted on the ground, are grinding corn into a coarse meal for the atole, or mush. At the zanja several are engaged in washing clothes. Here these girls live under the care of an old Indian woman, and unless she accompanies them they may not, until they are married, go outside these walls. Near the mission we visit a long row of small adobe buildings, the homes of the families of the Christian Indians; a neat, busy settlement where the little ones, comfortably clothed, play about attended by the older children, while the mothers work for the padres four or five hours daily.

Leaving San Diego and traveling northward along "El Camino Real," the highway which leads from mission to mission, we reach San Luis Rey, "King of the Missions," as it is sometimes called. Its church is the largest of all those erected by the padres, being one hundred and sixty feet long, fifty-eight feet wide, and sixty feet high. Its one square, two-story tower has a chime of bells, the sweet clear tones of which reached our ears while we were yet miles from the mission. Counting the arches of the long corridor, we find there are two hundred and fifty-six. This mission became very wealthy. At one time it had a baptized Indian population of several thousand, owned twenty-four thousand cattle, ten thousand horses, and one hundred thousand sheep, and harvested fourteen thousand bushels of grain a year.

Its prosperity was due in a great measure to good Padre Peyri, who had charge of it from its beginning. Many years afterwards, as we shall see, the padres were ordered by the Mexican government to leave their missions, the wealth they had gathered, and the Indians they had taught and cared for. Father Peyri, knowing how hard it would be for him to get away from his Indian children, as he called them, slipped off by night to San Diego. In the morning the Indians missed him. Learning what had happened, five hundred of them mounted their ponies in hot haste and galloped all the way to San Diego, forty-five miles, to bring him back by force. They arrived just as the ship, with Padre Peyri on board, was weighing anchor. Standing on deck with outstretched arms, the padre blessed them amid their tears and loud cries. Some flung themselves into the water and swam after the ship. Four reached it, and, climbing up its sides, so implored to be taken on board that the padre consented and carried them with him to Rome, where one afterwards became a priest.

The next link in our chain, the most beautiful of all the missions, is that of San Juan Capistrano. It was founded in 1776, the year of our Declaration of Independence, but in 1812 it was destroyed by an earthquake, the massive towers and noble arch falling in on the Indians, who were assembled in the church for morning prayers. Many of them were killed. The church has never been rebuilt.

It is Christmas Day when we reach San Gabriel, the next station on El Camino Real. Inside the great cactus fence which incloses the square about the mission we see a strangely mixed company,--Indians in their best clothes, their faces shining from a liberal use of mission soap and water; soldiers in their leather suits freshened up for the holiday; a few ranchmen in the gay dress of the times, riding beautiful horses; women and girls each brilliant in a bright-colored skirt with shawl or scarf gracefully draped over head and shoulders.

The Christmas Day morning service, held at four o'clock and known by the common people as the Rooster Mass, is long since over. The crowd is now gathered for the Pastorel, which, like the miracle plays of the Middle Ages, is a drama with characters taken from the Bible.

First to appear on the scene is an orchestra composed of young Indians playing violins, bass viols, reeds, flutes, and guitars. Closely following come the actors, representing San Gabriel and attendant angels, Satan, Blind Bartimeus, and a company of shepherds. The entertainment is very simple. There is the announcement of the birth of the Savior, the adoration of the babe, and the offering of gifts. The play concludes with a protracted struggle between San Gabriel and Satan for the possession of Blind Bartimeus, in which the saint finally comes off victor while the orchestra plays lively music. After the Pastorel there are games, dancing, and feasting. Every one seems happy, and it is with regret that we leave the gay scene.

Through the hills to the north, across the Arroyo Seco, not dry now, but a swift stream turbulent from the winter rains, we journey on. We pass Eagle Rock, a great bowlder high upon the green hillside, one of the landmarks of the region, and enter the valley of the Los Angeles River. After traveling for several hours, we come to a large plantation of trees, vines, and grainfields, in the midst of which lies the mission of San Fernando. Its land extends for miles on every side and is exceedingly fertile. In front of the beautiful cloisters, under tall and stately palm trees, a fountain sends high its sparkling water, which falls back with pleasant tinkle into a basin of carved stone.

When we reach San Buenaventura, the next mission on our route, we find priests and Indians exceedingly busy, for word has come from Monterey that a Yankee trading vessel will soon sail for the south, and cattle must be killed and the fat rendered into tallow for the market. As hides and tallow are about the only commodities the padres have for sale, this is an important event. Indians tend the caldrons of bubbling grease, and keep up the fires under the kettles. When the tallow is slightly cooled, they pour it into sacks made from the skins of animals. These, when filled with the hardened tallow, look as though each again held a plump beast.

Traveling up the coast we come one afternoon to

A golden bay 'neath soft blue skies Where on a hillside creamy rise The mission towers whose patron saint Is Barbara--with legend quaint.

Here spring is merging into summer, and we are in time to see the ceremony which closes the wheat harvest. The workmen gather the last four sheaves from the field, and, fastening them in the form of a cross, carry them, followed by a long procession of dusky reapers, up the ascent to the church. As they approach, the bells burst out in a joyous peal, and from the mission doors the padres come forth, one bearing a cross, another the banner of the Virgin. A choir of Indian boys follows, chanting a hymn. All advance slowly down the avenue to meet the sheaf bearers, then counter march to the church, where the harvest festival is celebrated.

Passing by other missions, we must close our journey with a visit to San Carlos, the Monterey mission, most prominent of all in the history of the church and state. It was from the first the special charge of Padre Junipero Serra, and, at the time we see it, his monument as well; for in it at last his weary body was laid to rest beside his friend Padre Juan Crespi, to whose writings, next to those of Padre Francisco Palou, we are most indebted for our knowledge of Junipero Serra and his great work. In 1813, with its graceful arched front and two towers, San Carlos was a noble-looking building, but since that time one tower has fallen.

We are reminded, as we look, of the scene when Junipero lay dying. Ever since morning the grief-stricken people had been waiting, listening for the news from the sick room. When the tolling of the bell announced that the beautiful life was ended, crowds came weeping and lamenting, anxious to see again the beloved face.

It was with great difficulty that the Indians could be kept from tearing the padre's robe from his body, so earnestly did they desire to possess some relic of the father they had loved so long.

Here we notice the daily life of the Indian, which (in 1813) is the same at all the missions. At sunrise comes the sound of the bells calling to the morning prayers, and we see the natives hurrying to the church. After service they gather for breakfast of mush and tortillas. As the flocks and herds have increased, meat forms part of the daily food, sometimes from the freshly killed beeves, but generally in a dried state called carne seco. After breakfast the workers go in groups to their various employments. Dinner is served at eleven, and they have a resting period until two. Then work is again taken up and continued until an hour before sunset, when the bells call to evening prayer. Supper follows the evening service, after which the Indians can do as they like until bedtime. We see some engaged in a game of ball. Many are squatted on the ground playing other games,--gambling, we suspect. In one group there is dancing to the music of violin and guitar. There is laughter and chattering on all sides, and to us they seem happy, at least for the time.

The life led by the Indians at the missions was not generally a hard one. No doubt when they first came, or were brought, into the settlements, from their free wild life, they found it harder to keep the regular hours of the missions than to perform the work, which was seldom very heavy. When disobedient or lazy, they were punished severely, judging by the standards of to-day, but really no harder than was at that time the custom in schools and in navies the world over. When the soldiers came in contact with the natives, there was generally cruel treatment for the latter. But as far as possible the padres stood between their charges and the soldiers, always placing the mission as far from the presidio as the safety of the former would allow.

At San Diego, about five years after its settlement, wild Indians surprised the mission guard, and killed the padre and several of the converted Indians in a most cruel manner. The Spanish government gave orders that the murderers should be taken and executed and this mission abandoned; but Padre Junipero begged so hard for the culprits, who, he said, knew no better, having no knowledge of God, that he was finally allowed to have his way. Gentleness and patience won the day; not only the Indians who made the attack were converted, but many more of their tribe, and the mission became a flourishing settlement. There was once a rebellion among the Santa Clara and San Jose Indians, led by a young convert from Santa Clara, which required soldiers from Monterey to put down. Generally, however, the mission life was peaceful, the Indians being fond of their padres.

When Mexico became free from Spain, no more money was sent up to pay the soldiers or run the government in Upper California, and for a long time the missions advanced the money for the expenses of the government.

After a time the new priests who came up from Mexico were not generally men of such education and noble character as the early mission padres. They cared less for missionary work, and were not so energetic. Their influence was not always good for the Indians, who quickly saw the difference between them and their old padres. They had little confidence in the newcomers, so at the few missions where such as these were in charge the Indians were disobedient, and received harsh punishments from the padres; and trouble followed.

In 1833 the Mexican government decided to confirm the mandate issued by Spain several years before in regard to the breaking up of the mission settlements. By this law each Indian was to have his own piece of land to own and care for. He was to be no longer under the control of the church, but to be his own master like any other citizen. As for the padres, they were to give up their wealth and lands, and leave for other missionary fields. That this would create a great change in California all realized; still it was no new idea, but the plan Spain had in mind when the missions were first founded. The mistake was in supposing that it was possible for a people to rise in so short a time from the wild life of the California Indian to the position of self-supporting citizens in a civilized country.

When the Indians understood this order, some were pleased and, like children when freed from restraint, ceased to work and became troublesome. Many, however, when they found that the padres were to leave them, became very unhappy; some, it is said, even died from homesickness for the mission and the padre. One committed suicide.

It was soon seen that they were not fitted to look after themselves. Only a few years had passed since they were savages, knowing nothing of civilized life, and they still needed some one to guide them. They not only began to drink and gamble, but were cheated and ill-treated on all sides, until many of them became afraid of living in towns and went back to wild life. For this they were no longer fitted, and they suffered so much from hunger and cold that great numbers of them died.

Because the Indians were not capable of caring for themselves at the time of the secularization of the missions, the padres are often severely blamed. It is said that they tried to keep the natives without knowledge, in fact something like slaves. But the truth is that the padres taught them by thousands, not only to cultivate the soil, to irrigate wisely, to raise domestic cattle, but to work at every trade that could be of use in a new country. They were encouraged to choose from among themselves alcaldes, or under officers of the mission. In this way every inducement was given to the Indian showing himself capable of self-control, to rise to a prominent position in his little world, where he generally ruled his fellow-workmen wisely and kindly.

Added to this, the Indians acquired, through the teaching and example of the padres, a religion that has lasted through generations. The breaking up of the mission settlements scattered the Indians through the country, many of them going back to the wild life in the forest and mountains, where they no longer had any religious instructions. Yet to-day, after all the years that have passed, there are few Indians from San Diego to San Francisco who do not speak the language of the padres and follow, though it may be but feebly, the teaching of the Catholic faith, the "Santa Fe" of the padres.

Some of the mission buildings, many of the flocks, and much of the land fell into the hands of men who had no possible right to them. Orchards and vineyards were cut down, cattle killed and stolen, and there was only ruin where a short time before there had been thousands of busy people leading comfortable lives. Soon the churches were neglected and began to crumble away, bats flew in and out of the broken arches, squirrels chattered fearlessly in the padre's dining room, and the only human visitor was some sad-hearted Indian worshiper, slipping timidly into the desolate building to kneel alone before the altar where once

Sweet strains from dusky neophytes Rose up to God in praise, When life centered 'round the missions In the happy golden days.

Chapter V
Pastoral Days

For hundreds of years poets have written and singers have sung of the loveliness of a country life, where there is no gathering together of the inhabitants in great cities, no struggle to make money, where the people live much out of doors, are simple in their tastes, healthy and happy.

These dreams of an ideal life the Spanish-speaking settlers of early California made real. In this land of balmy airs, soft skies, and gentle seas there lived, in the old days, a people who were indifferent to money, who carried their religion into their daily pleasures and sorrows, were brotherly toward one another, contented, beautiful, joyous.

About the time that the mission of San Francisco was founded, the Spanish government decided to lay out two towns, or pueblos, where it was thought the fertile character of the soil would lead the settlers to raise grain and other supplies, not only for themselves but for the people of the presidios. Up to this time a large part of the food had been brought, at a considerable cost, from Mexico.

We know that the governor, Felipe de Neve, chose the town sites with care, for in the whole state there are nowhere more beautiful and fertile spots than San Jose, near the southern end of San Francisco Bay, and Los Angeles, near the famous valley of the San Gabriel River. In founding these two pueblos, and a third which was located where Santa Cruz now stands, the plan pursued was interesting and somewhat different from the methods of settlement on the eastern coast of our country.

First there was chosen a spot for the plaza, or central square, care being taken that it was not far from good grazing land suitable for the settlers' stock. Around the plaza, lots were set apart for the courthouse, town hall, church, granaries, and jail. Next were the lots for the settlers, who each had, besides his home spot, several acres of farming land with water, and the right to use the pasture lands of the town. To each family was given, also, two horses, two cows, two oxen, a mule, several goats, sheep, chickens, farming implements, and a small sum in money.

Instead of asking tax money of the town people, some of the land was reserved as public property to be rented out, the proceeds to be used for the expenses of the government. Many people believe that this is the wisest plan man has yet discovered for managing the expenses of a city, town, or country.

Los Angeles had for many years a large amount of this land near the center of the town, belonging to the city government. Gradually it was taken up by settlers or appropriated by officials until, when the place grew large and thriving, it was found that the land had become private property; and finally the city had to pay large sums for parks and land for public buildings.

Each pueblo was ruled by an alcalde, or mayor, and council, chosen by the people. To advise with these officers, there was a commissioner who represented the governor of the country. During the first few years the pueblo was governed largely by the commissioner. Presidios, which were, at first, forts with homes for the commander, officers, soldiers, and their families, and were ruled by the commanding officer or comandante, gradually became towns; and then they, too, had their alcalde and council. There were four presidios--Monterey, San Francisco, San Diego, and Santa Barbara.

In spite of all the gifts of free land, stock, and money, it was hard to secure a suitable class of settlers. Many of those who came up from Mexico to live in the pueblos were idle or dissipated, and nearly all uneducated. When, after several years, a Spanish officer was sent down from Monterey to convey to the Los Angeles settlers full title to their lands, he found that not one of the twenty-four heads of families could sign his name. Later a much better class of people came into the country --men of education, brave, hardy members of good Spanish families, who obtained grants of land from the government, bought cattle from the mission herds, and began the business of stock raising.

This was the beginning of the pastoral or shepherd life. Each rancho was miles in extent, its cattle and horses numbered by thousands. The homes were generally built around a court into which all the rooms opened, and were constructed of adobe bricks such as were used at the missions. In the better class of homes several feet of the space in the courtyard next the wall were covered with tile roofing, forming a shaded veranda, where the family were accustomed to spend the leisure hours. Here they received visitors, the men smoked their cigaritos, and the children made merry. In the long summer evenings sweet strains of Spanish music from violin and guitar filled the air, and the hard earthen floor of the courtyard resounded to the tap-tap of high-heeled slippers, the swish of silken skirts, and the jingle of silver spurs, as the young people took part in the graceful Spanish dances.

It was no small matter to rule one of these great households. La Patrona (the mistress) was generally the first one up. "Before the sun had risen," said a member of one of the old families, "while the linnets and mocking birds were sounding their first notes, my mother would appear at our bedside. 'Up, muchachos, up, muchachas, and kneel for your Alba!' The Alba was a beautiful prayer of thanksgiving for care during the night, with a plea for help through the dangers and temptations of the day. No excuse for lying abed was accepted; up, and on the floor we knelt, then she passed on to where the mayordomo, or foreman, and his men were gathering in the courtyard. Here, too, was the cook with the Indian maids, busy making tortillas for the morning meal. 'Your Albas, my children,' my mother would say in her clear, firm voice. Down would drop mayordomo, vaqueros, cook, and Indian girls, all devoutly reciting the morning prayer.

"After their prayer the children might, if they chose, return to their beds, but before sleep could again overtake them there would probably come from a distant room the voice of their aged grandfather asking them questions from the Spanish catechism.

"'Children, who made you?' he would call in a quavering voice.

"A chorus of small voices would sing-song in response, 'El Dios' [God].

"Again he would question, 'Children, who died for you?'

"Again the reply, 'El Dios.'

"By the time the questions were all answered there was no chance for more sleep."

Nothing was taken with the morning coffee but the tortilla. This was a thin cake made of meal from corn ground by Indian women who used for the grinding either a stone mortar and pestle, or a metate. The metate was a three-legged stone about two feet in length and one in breadth, slightly hollowed out in the center; grain was ground in this by rubbing with a smaller stone. It took a great number of tortillas to serve the large household. One Indian maid, kneeling beside a large white stone which served as table, mixed the meal, salt, and water into balls of dough. These she handed to another girl, who spatted them flat and thin by tossing them from one of her smooth bare arms to the other until they were but a little thicker than a knife blade. The cook then baked them on a hot dry stone or griddle, turning them over and over to keep them from burning.

El Patron (the master) usually rose early, and after his coffee, put on his high, wide-brimmed sombrero, and, attended by his sons, if they were old enough, and his mayordomo, rode over his estate, looking after the Indian vaqueros and workmen. One gentleman, a member of a fine Spanish family which lived in the southern part of the state, used to ride out with his sixteen sons, all of whom were over six feet in height. Generally the families were large, often comprising twelve children or more. These made merry households for the little people.

After breakfast it was the duty of the mistress to set the host of Indian girls to their tasks. The padres were always glad to let the young Indian girls from the mission go into white families where there was a wise mistress, that they might be trained in both religious and domestic duties. Going to the gate of the courtyard, the Patrona would call, "To the brooms, to the brooms, muchachas," adding, if it were foggy, "A very fine morning for the brooms, little ones;" and out would come running a cluster of Indian girls carrying each a broom. At the work they would go, sweeping as clean as a floor the courtyard and ground for a large space about the house.

Next they flocked to the sewing room, often sixteen or eighteen of these girls, to take up their day's work under the mistress's eye. Some made garments for the ranch hands, those who were better work women attended to the making of clothing for the family, while the girls who were the most skillful with the needle fashioned delicate, fine lace work and embroidery.

The children were seldom indoors unless it rained. There were no schools; there were few ranches where there were teachers, and the fathers and mothers generally had their hands too full to devote themselves to their children's education, so in the early days it was all playtime. Later, schools were started for boys, and dreadful places they were.

As General Vallejo describes them, they were generally held in a narrow, badly lighted room, with no adornment but a large green cross or some picture of a saint hanging beside the master's table. The master was often an old soldier in fantastic dress, with ill-tempered visage. The scholar entered, walked the length of the room, knelt before the cross or picture, recited a prayer, then tremblingly approached the master, saying, "Your hand, Senor Maestro," when with a grunt the hand would be extended to him to be kissed. Little was taught besides the reading of the primer and the catechism.

Ranch boys early learned to ride, each having his own horse and saddle. Every year there was a rodeo, or "round-up," held in each neighborhood, where cattle from all the surrounding ranches were driven to one point for the purpose of counting the animals and branding the young. Each stock owner had to be there with all the men from his ranch who could ride, nor must he forget his branding irons. These brands were recorded in the government book of the department, and any one changing the form of his iron in any manner without the permission of the judge was guilty of a crime.

To the boys the rodeo was the most interesting time of the whole year. The coming of the strange herds and vaqueros, the counting and the separating of the animals, and the branding of the young stock made a period of excitement and fun. Here was offered a chance for the display of good horsemanship. Sometimes as the cattle were being gradually herded into a circular mass, an unruly cow or bull would suddenly dart from the drove and run away at full speed. A vaquero on horseback would immediately dash after the animal, and, coming up with it, lean from the saddle and seizing the runaway by the tail, spur his horse forward. Then by a quick movement he would give a jerk and suddenly let go his hold, when the animal would fall rolling over and over on the ground. By the time it was up again it was tamed. Many a boy earned his first praise for good riding at a rodeo.

Nowhere in the world were there better and more graceful riders. Horses used for pleasure were fine, spirited animals. The saddle and the bridle were generally handsomely inlaid with silver or gold. A California gentleman in fiesta costume, mounted on his favorite horse, was a delight to the eyes. His hat, wide in the brim, high and pointed in the crown, was made of soft gray wool and ornamented with gold or silver lace and cord, sometimes embroidered with rubies and emeralds until it was very heavy and exceedingly valuable. His white shirt was of thin, embroidered muslin, and the white stock, too, was of thin stuff wrapped several times around the neck, then tied gracefully in front. The jacket was of cloth or velvet, in dark colors, blue, green, or black, with buttons and lace trimmings of silver or gold, often of a very elaborate design. About the waist was tied a wide sash of soft material and gay color, the ends hanging down at the side. The breeches were of velvet or heavy cloth, dark in color, save when the rider was gay in his taste, then they might be of bright tints. They either ended at the knee, below which were leggings of deerskin, or fitted the figure closely down to just above the ankle, where they widened out and were slashed at the outer seam, showing thin white drawers, which puffed prettily between the slashes. A gentleman in Los Angeles still has the trimmings for such suit, consisting of three hundred and fifty pieces of silver filigree work.

Every one seemed to live out of doors, and though the ranchos were widely scattered, there was much visiting and social gayety. All who could, traveled on horseback; while the mother of the family, the children, and old people used the clumsy carreta with its squeaking wheels.

One of the prettiest sights was a wedding procession as it escorted the bride from her home to the mission church. Horses were gayly caparisoned, and the riders richly dressed. The nearest relative of the bride carried her before him on the saddle, across which hung a loop of gold or silver braid for her stirrup, in which rested her little satin-shod foot. Her escort sat behind her on the bearskin saddle blanket. Accompanying the party were musicians playing guitar and violin, each managing horse and instrument with equal skill.

The California woman generally wore a full skirt of silk, satin, wool, or cotton, a loose waist of thin white goods, and, in cold weather, a short bolero jacket of as rich material as could be obtained. A bright-colored ribbon served for a sash, and a lace handkerchief or a muslin scarf was folded over the shoulders and neck. In place of bonnet and wrap a lace or silk shawl, or a narrow scarf called a rebosa, was gracefully draped over the head and shoulders.

Children were dressed like the older people, and very pretty were the girls in their low-necked, short-sleeved camisas or waists, and full gay skirts, their hair in straight braids hanging down over the shoulders. The short breeches, pretty round jackets, and gay sashes were very becoming to the boys.

At night the daughters of the house, big and little, were locked into their rooms by their mother, the father attending in the same manner to the boys. In the morning the mother's first duty was to unlock these doors.

Various games were played. Blindman's buff was a great favorite for moonlight nights. There was also a game called cuatrito, in which the players threw bits of stone at a mark drawn on the ground at a certain distance.

"In my time," said a prominent Californian of to-day, "we used to play this game with golden slugs instead of stones; there was always a basket of slugs sitting door. We liked them because they carried well, and we thought it nothing unusual to use them as playthings. They were abundant in most of the houses; my mother and her friends used them as soap dishes in, the bedrooms.

"In the spare rooms was always a little pile of money covered by a napkin, from which the visitor was expected to help himself if he needed. We would have considered it disgraceful to count the guest money."

"Our parents were very strict with us," said another Californian, "much more so than is the custom to-day. Sometimes while the parents, brothers, and sisters were eating their meal, a child who was naughty had for punishment to kneel in one corner of the dining room before a high stool, on which was an earthen plate, a tin cup, and a wooden spoon. It was worse than a flogging, a thousand times. As soon as the father went out, the mother and sisters hastened to the sorrowful one and comforted him with the best things from the table."

The clothes were not laundered each week, but were saved up often for several weeks or even a month or two, and then came a wash-day frolic. Imagine wash day looked forward to as a delightful event! So it was, however, to many California children. Senorita Vallejo, in the Century Magazine (Vol. 41), thus describes one of these excursions:--

"It made us children happy to be waked before sunrise to prepare for the 'wash-day expedition.' The night before, the Indians had soaped the clumsy carreta's great wheels. Lunch was placed in baskets, and the gentle oxen were yoked to the pole. We climbed in under the green cloth of an old Mexican flag which was used as an awning, and the white-haired Indian driver plodded beside with his long oxgoad. The great piles of soiled linen were fastened on the backs of horses led by other servants, while the girls and women who were to do the washing trooped along by the side of the carreta. Our progress was slow, and it was generally sunrise before we reached the spring. The steps of the carreta were so low that we could climb in or out without stopping the oxen. The watchful mother guided the whole party, seeing that none strayed too far after flowers, or loitered too long. Sometimes we heard the howl of coyotes and the noise of other wild animals, and then none of the children were allowed to leave the carreta.

"A great dark mountain rose behind the spring, and the broad, beautiful valley, unfenced and dotted with browsing herds, sloped down to the bay [of San Francisco]. We watched the women unload the linen and carry it to the spring, where they put home-made soap on the clothes, dipped them in the spring, and rubbed them on the smooth rocks until they were white as snow. Then they were spread out to dry on the tops of the low bushes growing on the warm, windless southern slopes of the mountain." After a happy day in the woods came "the late return at twilight, when the younger children were all asleep in the slow carreta and the Indians were singing hymns as they drove the linen-laden horses down the dusky ravines."

As at the missions, soon the ranchos, little was raised for sale save hides and tallow from the cattle. It was not the fault of the settlers that, living in so fertile a country, they made so little use of its productiveness. Spain's laws in regard to trade were made entirely in the interests of the mother country, the settlers of New Spain, especially of Alta California, having no encouragement to raise more than they needed for use at home. They could not sell their produce to ships from foreign countries, for the penalty for that was death to the foreigner and severe punishment for the colonist. All trade had to be carried on in Spanish vessels, and it was forbidden to ship olive oil, wine, or anything that was raised or made in the home country. As California and Spain were much alike in climate and soil, this law really stopped all outside trade except that arising from cattle.

After the territory became a Mexican province, the rules were not so severe in regard to foreign trade, and finally the New England vessels freely entered the ports by paying certain duties to the government.

To the young people upon the ranchos the arrival of a trading vessel was a great event. If the port was not far from the house, the Patrona and the young ladies sometimes went on board to select for themselves from the miscellaneous cargo the things they desired; but as they were generally afraid of the water, especially of trusting themselves in the ship's boats, the father and boys often represented the family on such occasions.

When news arrived that a ship was coming down the coast, elder sisters became very kind and attentive to younger brothers, who accepted panocha (a coarse brown sugar cast in square or scalloped cakes) and other gifts contentedly, knowing well they would be expected to "coax Father" to buy the ring, sash, necklace, or fan which the good sister particularly desired. Often a ranchero would go down to the harbor with ten or fifteen ox carts loaded with hides, skins, and tallow, and return with ranch implements, furniture, dishes, sugar, other food, clothes, and ornaments of all kinds. Such laughing, chattering, and excitement as there was when the squeaking ox carts came into the courtyard! The whole household, from the Patrona and her guests to the Indian mothers with their children from the kitchen precincts, gathered to watch the slow unloading of the purchases. Slow, indeed, seemed the process to the eager children of the family. Except on horseback for a short dash, the Californian never hurried. For a journey the usual gait was a little jog trot, hardly faster than a walk.

Senorita Vallejo, in the Century Magazine, describes the loading of a ship's cargo: "The landing place for the mission of San Jose was at the mouth of a salt water creek several miles away. When a trading vessel entered San Francisco Bay, the large ship's boat would be sent up this creek to collect the hides and tallow; but if the season was a wet one, the roads would be too bad for the ox carts; then each separate hide was doubled across the middle and placed on the head of an Indian. Sometimes long files of Indians might be seen, each carrying hides in this manner, as they trotted across the wide, flat plains or pushed their way through the little forest of dried mustard stalks to the creek mouth."

No such thing was known as a Californian breaking his word in regard to a debt. Yankee ship owners trusted him freely. Once, when a ship was in port, the captain left it for a little while in charge of the clerk whose business it was to sell the goods, but who had never been in California before and knew nothing of its customs. Down to the shore came a ranchero attended by servants and ox carts. He came on board and bought many things, intending to pay later with hides and tallow which were not then ready. When he ordered the goods taken ashore with never a word as to payment, the clerk informed him that he must either give money or else give some writing saying that he would pay.

Now this Californian, though rich in lands and stock, could neither read nor write. When he understood that he was being distrusted, he gravely drew from his beard a hair, and, handing it to the clerk, said: "Give this to your master and tell him it is a hair from the beard of Agustin Machado. You will find it sufficient guarantee." The clerk saw that he had made a mistake, and, taking the hair, placed it in the leaves of his note book and allowed the goods to be taken away. When the captain returned, he was mortified that there had been any distrust shown.

While California was a Spanish province its chief ruler was appointed by the home government and was always an educated gentleman of good family, generally an officer of the army. The coming of a new governor was a great event in the colony and was celebrated with all possible ceremony and display.

In 1810 Mexico began its revolt against Spain. In California the people were in sympathy with the mother country and had no doubt of her final success. For a long time they received little news of how the war was progressing. They only knew that no more money was sent up to pay the soldiers or the expenses of government, that the padres no longer received any income from the Pius Fund, that even the trading vessels from Mexico upon which they depended for their supplies had ceased to come.

Times became so hard that the local government turned for aid to the missions, which had become largely self-supporting. Many of them were indeed wealthy communities, and the padres responded generously to the demand for help. For several years they furnished food and clothing to the soldiers, and money for the expenses of government, for the most of which they never received payment.

Gradually the fine clothes of the Californians wore out, no vessels arrived from which they could purchase more, and again it was the missions which came to the rescue. Their cotton and woolen goods were in great demand. Indian spinners and weavers were busy from morning until night making clothes for the "gente de razon," or "people of reason," which was the term by which the white settlers were distinguished from the natives.

In 1822 a vessel came up from the south, bringing to the governor official notice that the war had been decided in favor of Mexico, and that California was therefore a Mexican province. This was disagreeable news to the Californians, but after consultation held by the governor, his officers, the padre who was the president of the missions, and some of the leading citizens, it was decided that they were too far away from Spain to be able to resist, and that they should take the oath to be true to the Mexican government. For the padres, who were all Spaniards and loyal to the home government, this was a hard thing to do, and they never became reconciled to the change.

From this time California was not so well governed. Mexico, which was then an empire but soon became a republic, had its hands full looking after its own affairs, and little attention was paid its far-off province. Its best men were needed at home, and the governors sent up the coast were not always wise or pleasing to the people. There were several revolutions with but little bloodshed. One governor was sent back to Mexico. At one time the Californians declared that theirs was a free state, and a young man named Alvarado was made governor. General Vallejo, who was his uncle, was given command of the army. But soon the Californians quarreled bitterly among themselves, so that this government did not last long and the territory went back under the rule of Mexico. That government, in order to have peace in the province, confirmed Alvarado and Vallejo in their positions.

During the war between Mexico and Spain a South American pirate paid a visit to the coast of Upper California. Monterey was attacked and partly destroyed, also the mission of San Juan Capistrano and the rancho El Refugio, the home of Captain Ortega, the discoverer of San Francisco Bay. In the crew of the pirate ship was a young American named Chapman, who had found life among his rough associates not so interesting as he had hoped it would be, so he deserted, but was taken prisoner by the Californians and imprisoned in a canyon near the present site of Pasadena. Later he was brought down to Los Angeles and set at liberty. He found the people of the pueblo planning to build a church on the plaza, and he told them that if they would let him have some Indian workmen he would get some large timbers down from the canyon. He accomplished this successfully, and it was considered a wonderful work. The stumps of the trees can yet be seen far up on the mountain side, and the timbers are still in the plaza church.

Visiting San Gabriel, young Chapman found the padres having trouble to keep the flour which they ground in their new stone mill from being dampened by water from the mill wheel. Knowing something of machinery, the American remedied the defect by means of a flutter wheel, and there was no more trouble.

For years the catching of otters for their fur along the lagoons and bays about San Francisco and Monterey brought considerable money to the northern missions. Chapman, finding that the padres of San Gabriel were anxious to engage in this trade, built for them the first sea-going boat ever constructed in southern California. It was a schooner, the various parts of which he made in the workshop of the mission. They were then carried down to San Pedro, where he put them together and successfully launched the vessel.

Finally, to close his history, it is recorded of Mr. Chapman that he fell in love with the pretty daughter of Captain Ortega, whose home he had helped his pirate associates to attack, that he married her and lived to a good old age. The country had few more useful citizens than this capable man, the first American to settle in the southern part of California.

With the secularization of the missions in 1833-34 came a change in the peaceful pastoral life. In each section all that was of interest had from the first centered around its mission. One of the chief pleasures of the early Californians was the feast day, "La Fiesta," which celebrated a saint's birthday. During the year there were many of these festivals. First there were religious exercises at the mission church; then in the great square there followed dancing, games, and feasting, in which all classes took some part. These happy church festivals ceased with the breaking up of the mission settlements. Some of the Indians disturbed the community by disorderly conduct, and the ill treatment and suffering of the rest of these simple people caused sorrow and dismay in the hearts of the better portion of the settlers. There was a wild scramble for the lands, stock, and other wealth which had been gathered by the missionaries and their Indian workmen.

Many of the beautiful churches were sold to people who cared nothing for the faith they represented. In some, cattle were stabled. The mission bells were silent, and many of the mission settlements, once so busy and prosperous, were solitary and in ruins.

Life in the great ranchos still went on much as before, but it was no longer so simple and joyous. A change had begun, and not many years later, with the coming of the Americans at the time of the Mexican war, the peaceful, happy life of Spanish California was brought to an end.

Chapter VI
The Footsteps of the Stranger

At no point does the early history of California come in contact with that of the colonies of the Eastern coast of the United States. The nearest approach to such contact was in the year 1789, when Captain Arguello, commander of the presidio of San Francisco, received the following orders from the governor of the province:--

"Should there arrive at your port a ship named Columbia, which, they say, belongs to General Washington of the American States, you will take measures to secure the vessel with all the people aboard with discretion, tact, cleverness, and caution." As the Columbia failed to enter the Californian port, the Spanish commander had no chance to try his wits and guns with those of the Yankee captain.

It would seem as though the Californians lived for a time in fear of their Eastern neighbors, since prayers were offered at some of the missions that the people be preserved from "Los Americanos;" but after the coming of the first two or three American ships, when trade began to be established, there arose the kindliest feeling between the New England traders and the Californians. The ship Otter, from Boston, which came to the coast in 1796, was the first vessel from the United States to anchor in a California port.

La Perouse, in command of a French scientific expedition, was the first foreigner of prominence to visit California. Of his visit, which occurred in the fall of 1786, he writes in his journal: "The governor put into the execution of his orders in regard to, us a graciousness and air of interest that merits from us the liveliest acknowledgments, and the padres were as kind to us as the officers. We were invited to dine at the Mission San Carlos, two leagues from Monterey, were received upon our arrival there like lords of a parish visiting their estates. The president of the missions, clad in his robe, met us at the door of the church, which was illuminated as for the grandest festival. We were led to the foot of the altar and the Te Deum chanted in thanksgiving for the happy issue of our voyage."

La Perouse's account of the country, the people, and the missions is of great value in giving us a picture of these times. In regard to the Indians he said that he wished the padres might teach them, besides the principles of the Christian religion, some facts about law and civil government, "Although," said he, "I admit that their progress would be very slow, the pains which it would be necessary to take very hard and tiresome."

Captain Vancouver, with two vessels of the British navy, bound on an exploring voyage round the world, was the next stranger to visit, California. So much did he enjoy the courtesy of the Spanish officers that when his map of the coast came out it was found that he had honored his hosts of San Francisco and Monterey by naming for them two leading capes of the territory, one Point Arguello and the other Point Sal.

As early as 1781 Russia had settlements in Sitka and adjacent islands, for the benefit of its fur traders, and in 1805 the Czar sent a young officer of his court to look into the condition of these trading posts. Count Rezanof found the people suffering and saw that unless food was brought to them promptly, they would die from starvation. San Francisco was the nearest port, and though he knew that Spain did not allow trade with foreign countries, the Russian determined to make the attempt to get supplies there. Loading a vessel with goods which had been brought out for the Indian trade of the north coast, he sailed southward. The story of his visit is well told by Bret Harte in his beautiful poem, "Concepcion de Arguello."

Rezanof was warmly welcomed and generously entertained by Commander Arguello of the presidio of San Francisco, but in vain did he try to trade off his cargo for food for his starving people. The governor and his officers dared not disobey the laws of Spain in regard to foreign trade. While they were arguing and debating, however, something happened which changed their views. The Count fell in love with the commander's beautiful daughter, Concepcion. Then, as the poem has it,--

". . . points of gravest import yielded slowly one by one, And by Love was consummated what Diplomacy begun."

It seemed to the governor that the man who was to be son-in-law in the powerful family of Arguello could not be considered as a foreigner, and therefore the law need not apply in his case. Thus the Count got his ship load of food and sailed away, promising to return as soon as possible for his betrothed wife. One of the most interesting pictures of early California is the poem which tells of this pathetic love story.

Count Rezanof was so pleased with the beauty and fertility of California that his letters interested the Czar, who decided to found a colony on the coast. An exploring expedition was sent out, and the territory about Russian River in Sonoma County was purchased of the Indians for three blankets, three pairs of trousers, two axes, three hoes, and some beads. Fort Ross was the main settlement, and was the home of the governor, his officers and their families, all accomplished, intelligent men and women. Besides the soldiers there were a number of mechanics and a company of natives from the Aleutian Islands, who were employed by the Russians to hunt the otter. Up and down the coast roamed these wild sea hunters, even collecting their furry game in San Francisco Bay and defying the comandante of the presidio, who had no boats with which to pursue them, and so could do nothing but fume and write letters of remonstrance to the governor of Fort Ross. Spain, and later Mexico, looked with disfavor and suspicion upon the Russian settlement, but the people of California were always ready for secret trade with their northern neighbors.

In 1816 Otto von Kotzebue, captain of the Russian ship Rurik, visited San Francisco and was entertained by the comandante, Lieutenant Luis Arguello. With Captain Kotzebue was the German poet, Albert von Chamisso.

The Russian captain, with brighter faith and keener insight than any other of the early visitors to the coast, says of the country: "It has hitherto been the fate of these regions to remain unnoticed; but posterity will do them justice; towns and cities will flourish where all is now desert; the waters over which scarcely a solitary boat is yet seen to glide will reflect the flags of all nations; and a happy, prosperous people receiving with thankfulness what prodigal nature bestows for their use will dispense her treasures over every part of the world."

In the writings of Albert von Chamisso can be found a most interesting description of his visit. To him is due the honor of giving to our Californian poppy its botanical name.

In 1841, the supply of otter having become exhausted, the Russians sold their property and claims about Fort Ross to the Swiss emigrant, the genial John Sutter. In 1903, through the agency of the Landmarks Society, this property and its still well-preserved buildings came into the possession of the state of California.

As early as 1826 there were a number of foreigners settled in California. These were mostly men from Great Britain or the United States who had married California women and lived and often dressed like their Spanish-speaking neighbors. Captain John Sutter, the Swiss who bought out the Russians of Fort Ross, came to California in 1839. He obtained from the Mexican government an extensive grant of land about the present site of Sacramento, and here he erected the famous Sutter's Fort where all newcomers, were made welcome and, if they desired, given work under this kindest of masters. Around the fort, which was armed with cannon bought from the Russians, he built a high stockade. He gained the good will of the Indians and had their young men drilled daily in military tactics by a German officer.

Governor Alvarado, at the time of his revolution in 1837, had in his forces, under a leader named Graham, a company of wandering Americans, trappers and hunters of the roughest type. Although there was no real war, and no fighting occurred, yet when Alvarado and his party were successful, Graham and his men demanded large rewards, and because the governor would not satisfy them they began to persecute him in every way possible. Alvarado says: "I was insulted at every turn by the drunken followers of Graham; when I walked in my garden they would climb on the wall and call upon me in terms of the greatest familiarity, 'Ho, Bautista, come here, I want to speak to you.' It was 'Bautista' here, 'Bautista' there."

To express dissatisfaction they held meetings in which they talked loudly about their country's getting possession of the land, until Governor Alvarado, having good reason to believe that they were plotting a revolution, expelled them from the territory and sent them to Mexico.

The United States took up the defense of the exiles and insisted on their being returned to California. It does not seem that the better class of Americans who had been long residents of the country sympathized with Graham and his followers, but from this time there were less kindly relations between the Californians and the citizens of the United States who came into the territory.

We come now to the story of the conquest.

At the beginning of the year 1845 the United States and Mexico were on the verge of war over Texas, which had been formerly a Mexican province, but through the influence of American settlers had rebelled, declaring itself an independent state, and had applied for admission to the American Union. Because the question of slavery was concerned in this application, it caused intense excitement throughout the United States. The South was determined to have the new territory come in as a slave-holding state, while the men of the North opposed the annexation of another acre of slave land.

Eight Northern legislatures protested against its admission. Twelve leading senators of the North declared that "it would result in the dissolution of the United States and would justify it." On the other hand, the South resolved that "it would be better to be out of the Union with Texas than in it without her." The South won its point. Texas was admitted, and at once a dispute with Mexico arose over the boundary lines, and war at length followed, being brought on in a measure by the entrance of United States troops into the disputed territory. During the long discussion over Texas the United States was having trouble with Great Britain over Oregon, which was then the whole country lying between the Mexican province of California and the Russian possessions on the north coast (now Alaska). Before the invention of steam cars and the construction of railroads, the Pacific coast region had been thought of little value. The popular idea was expressed by Webster when he said: "What do we want of this vast, worthless area, this region of savages and wild beasts, of deserts, of shifting sands and whirlwinds of dust, of cactus and prairie dogs?" But now the United States was waking up, and things looked different. Of Oregon the Americans were determined to have at least a portion. California, so far away from Mexico and so poorly governed, they would like to take under their protection,--at least the region around the great Bay of San Francisco.

As early as 1840 the United States government urged its consul at Monterey, an American named Larkin, secretly to influence the leading Californians to follow the example of Texas, secede from Mexico, and join the United States, where he was to assure them they would receive a brother's welcome. Just as he felt he might be successful his plans were overthrown.

One morning in 1842 there came sailing into Monterey Bay two American men-of-war. Suddenly, to the consternation of those watching from the shore, one of the ships was seen to fire upon an outgoing Mexican sloop. After making it captive the three vessels proceeded to the anchorage. Great was the excitement in Monterey. Neither the comandante nor the American consul could imagine the reason for such strange conduct. It was soon explained, however, by the arrival of a ship's boat bringing an officer who delivered to the authorities a demand for the surrender of the fort and place to the American commander of the Pacific fleet, Commodore Jones, who was on board one of the newly arrived vessels.

The Mexican officials and the officers of the army were astonished; so, too, was the United States consul. They knew of no war between these countries. Since he had neither men nor arms to resist this strange demand, Alvarado, who was acting for the absent governor, gave orders to surrender, and the next day the Mexican flag and forces gave place to those of the United States.

After the ceremony of taking possession, Commodore Jones had a talk with the American consul, Mr. Larkin, and learned to his dismay that the letters upon which he had acted and which indicated that war had been declared were misleading, and from the latest news it was evident that there was peace between the two countries.

The commodore saw at once that he had made a serious mistake, "a breach of the faith of nations," as it was called, which was liable to involve the United States in grave difficulties. How best to undo his rash action was now his thought.

He apologized to the Mexican commander and gave back possession of the fort. Next, he had the unhappy task of taking down the American flag and replacing it with the cactus and eagle banner of Mexico, to which the guns of his vessels gave a salute of honor. From Monterey he sailed away to San Pedro. There he waited while he sent a messenger to Governor Micheltorena, who was living in Los Angeles, asking permission to call upon him and apologize in person. This request was granted, and Commodore Jones and his staff came up to Los Angeles, where they were the guests of their countryman, Don Abel Stearns, who, as he had been working with Consul Larkin to win the Californians to the United States, was most anxious to undo the mischief of the flag raising. For the benefit of this history, Dona Arcadia Bandini, who was the beautiful Spanish wife of Mr. Stearns, tells the story of the visit:--

"We gave a dinner to the governor, the commodore, and their attendants. Everything was very friendly; they seemed to enjoy themselves, and the uniforms of the two countries were very handsome. On the next day but one the governor gave a ball. It was to be at his home, which was the only two-story house in Los Angeles. To show the Americans how patriotic the people of California were, the governor requested in the invitations that all the ladies wear white with a scarf of the Mexican colors,-- red, green, and white. Of course we gladly complied, though some of us had to work hard to get our costumes ready.

"The day of the ball came, but with it came rain, such a storm as I never had seen. As it drew toward evening the water came down faster and faster. The governor had the only carriage in California, and this he was to send for the commodore, Mr. Stearns, Isadora, and myself; but the poor young officers had to walk, and their faces were long when they looked out at the rain and then down at their fine uniforms and shining boots.

"Our California horses were not trained to pull loads and would not work in the rain, so when the carriage came for us it was drawn by a number of the governor's Cholo soldiers. We got in quite safely, and it was only a short distance we had to go, but as I was getting out the wind suddenly changed and down came a torrent of water on me. It was clear that I could not go to the ball in that condition, but the governor immediately ordered the soldiers to pull the carriage back to my home, where I soon made another toilet. The ball was delightful. The governor and the commodore vied with each other in exchanging compliments and courtesies."

It was a sad fact, however, that in spite of apologies, dinners, and balls, Consul Larkin now found it difficult to persuade his California neighbors that the United States looked upon them as brothers, and they began to regard with suspicion the host of American emigrants who were coming into the territory.

In 1842 Lieutenant Fremont, under orders from the United States government, made the first of his wonderful journeys over deserts and rough mountain ranges into the great unknown West. Soon he was to become famous, not only in his own country but in Europe, as the "Pathfinder," the road maker of the West. Already many an Oregon emigrant had blessed the name of Fremont for making plain the trail for himself and his loved ones.

In 1846 Captain Fremont, conducting an exploring and scientific expedition, entered California with sixty men and encamped in the valley of the San Joaquin. Later he moved down into the heart of the California settlements and encamped on the Salinas River. Possibly, knowing that war would soon be declared between his country and Mexico, he had determined to see as much of the enemy's position as possible, not caring particularly what the Mexican authorities might think.

As a natural result, General Castro, commander of the California forces, objected; Fremont defied him, and there seemed a likelihood of immediate war. There was no actual fighting, however, and in a day or two Fremont continued his journey toward Oregon.

He had gone but a little way when he was overtaken by a captain of the navy named Gillespie, bringing him letters from the officers of the government at Washington. Upon reading these, Fremont immediately turned about and marched swiftly back to Sutter's Fort, where he encamped. Just what orders the messages from Washington contained, no one knows; but it is thought that perhaps they informed Fremont that war would be declared very soon and that the government would be pleased if he could quietly get possession of California.

If this was so, he had the best of reasons for his later actions. If not, then in his eagerness to obtain for his country the valuable territory he so well appreciated and in his desire to win for himself the honor of gaining it, he brought on a war that caused the loss of many lives and much property, and the growth of a feeling of bitterness and distrust between Americans and Californians that has not yet entirely passed away. Still it is by no means certain that California could have been won without fighting, even had Fremont and the American settlers been more patient.

Soon many Americans were gathered about Fremont's camp; but though there were a number of rumors as to what General Castro was going to do to them, there was no action contrary to the previous kindly treatment all had received from the hands of the Californians. Still the emigrants felt that as soon as war was declared an army from Mexico might come up which would not be so considerate of them and their families as had been their California neighbors.

Having good reason to feel certain that Fremont would stand back of them if they began the fight, a company of Americans attacked one of Castro's officers, who, with a few men, was taking a band of horses to Monterey. Securing the horses, but letting the men who had them in charge get away, they hurried them to Fremont's camp, where they left them while they went on to Sonoma. Here they made prisoner General Vallejo, commander of that department of the territory, together with his brother and staff.

General Vallejo was one of the leading Californians of the north, a man of fine character, quiet and conservative, generous toward the needy emigrants and favorable to annexation with the United States. When he saw the rough character of the men surrounding his house that Sunday morning, he was at first somewhat alarmed. A man named Semple, who was one of the attacking party, describing the event in a Monterey paper sometime afterward, says: "Most of us were dressed in leather hunting shirts, many were very greasy, and all were heavily armed. We were about as rough a looking set of men as one could well imagine." When they assured the general that they were acting under orders from Fremont, he seemed to feel no more anxiety, gave up his keys, and arranged for the protection of the people of his settlement. He was first taken to Fremont's headquarters, then for safe keeping was sent on to Sutter's Fort.

Meanwhile the party which had been left in charge of affairs at Sonoma chose one of their number, a man named Ide, as their leader. Realizing that they had begun a war, they felt the need of a flag, and not daring to use that of the United States, they proceeded to make one for themselves. For their emblem they chose the strongest and largest of the animals of California, the grizzly bear. The flag was made of a Mexican rebosa or scarf of unbleached muslin about a yard in width and five feet long. To the bottom of this they sewed a strip of red flannel; in one corner they outlined a five-pointed star, and facing it a grizzly bear. These were filled in with red ink and under them in black letters were the words "California Republic." The temporary government of the followers of the Bear Flag is generally known as the "Bear Flag Republic."

As soon as it seemed probable that the Californians under General Castro were marching to attack the Americans, Captain Fremont joined his countrymen, and from that time the United States flag took the place of the banner of the bear. A little later Captain Fremont took the presidio and port of San Francisco, and to him is due the honor of naming beautiful Golden Gate.

About two weeks after the capture of Sonoma, Commodore Sloat, with two vessels of the United States navy, entered the harbor of Monterey. Although he had come for the purpose of taking the territory for his country, and had orders to see to it that England did not get possession of California ahead of him, yet he had been cautioned to deal kindly with the Californians, and he hesitated to take decided steps. It took him six days to make up his mind, and then he came to a decision partly on account of the actions of Fremont and his men. Slowly up the flagstaff on the fort of Monterey rose the Stars and Stripes. Unfolded by the sea breeze, the beautiful flag of the United States waved again over the land of the padres, and this time to stay. A few days later Commodore Stockton reached California to take command in place of Commodore Sloat, who returned home. Stockton appointed Fremont commander of the American forces on land, and together they completed the conquest of the territory.

It was unfortunate that Commodore Stockton had so lately arrived from the East that he did not fully understand the state of affairs. As he believed the wild rumors which, falsely, accused the Californians of treachery and cruelty, his proclamations were harsh and unjust to the proud but kindly people whom he was conquering. Many of the late historians find much to blame in the treatment given by the Americans to the people of California. Severity was often used when kindness would have had far better effect.

Los Angeles and San Diego were taken by Stockton and Fremont without any fighting, and leaving a few troops in the south, both commanders returned to

Monterey. They were soon recalled by the news that the people of Los Angeles had risen against the harsh rule of Captain Gillespie, who had been left in command; that the Americans had surrendered but had been allowed to retire to San Pedro, and that all the south was in a state of active rebellion.

Landing at San Pedro, Stockton waited a few days, then fearing the enemy was too strong for his forces, sailed away to San Diego. Here the Americans received a hearty welcome, and much-needed assistance, from the Spanish families of Bandini and Arguello.

Mr. Bandini escorted a body of the United States troops to his home rancho on the peninsula of Lower California, where he gave them cattle and other food supplies. For this aid to the invaders he was forced to remove his family from their home there, and on the journey up to San Diego. Mrs. Bandini made what was probably the first American flag ever constructed in California. As they neared San Diego the officer in command discovered that he had neglected to take with him a flag. He did not wish to enter the settlement without one, and when the matter was explained to Mrs. Bandini, who was journeying in a carreta with her maids and children, she offered to supply the need.

From the handbag on her arm came needle, thimble, thread, and scissors, and from the clothing of her little ones the necessary red, white, and blue cloth. Under the direction of the young officer she soon had a very fair-looking flag, and beneath its folds the party marched into the town. That night the band of the flagship Congress serenaded Mrs. Bandini in her San Diego home, and the next day Commodore Stockton called to thank her in person. The flag, it is said, he sent to Washington, where it is still to be found with other California trophies.

The most severe battle of the war in the state of California was fought on the San Pasqual rancho in San Diego County. The forces engaged were those of General Andres Pico, who commanded the Californians, and General Stephen Kearny, who had marched overland, entered the territory on the southwest, and was on his way to join Stockton. Hearing that the country was conquered and the fighting over, the American officer had sent back about two hundred of his men, but he was afterward reinforced by Captain Gillespie and fifty men sent by Stockton to meet him. Several American officers were killed in the battle of San Pasqual, and their brave commander severely wounded.

Commodore Stockton, on his march from San Diego to Los Angeles, twice engaged the enemy, once at the crossing of the San Gabriel River and once on the Laguna rancho just east of the city. The Californians behaved with great bravery. All of them were poorly armed, many having only lances and no fire-arms, and what powder they had was almost worthless; yet three times they dashed upon the square of steadily firing United States marines.

This was the last battle in the territory. The Californians retreated across the hills to the present site of Pasadena. Here, at the little adobe house on the banks of the Arroyo Seco, they separated. General Flores, their commander, was to ride with his staff through the stormy night, down El Camino Real toward Mexico. General Andres Pico, upon whom devolved the duty of surrender, was to ride with his associates to the old Cahuenga ranch house, the first station on the highway from Los Angeles to Santa Barbara. There he met Captain Fremont, and the treaty was signed which closed hostilities. The terms proposed by Fremont were favorable for the Californians and did much to make way for a peaceful settlement of all difficulties.

Chapter VII
At the Touch of King Midas

It was by chance that gold was discovered in both northern and southern California, and by chance that many great fortunes were made.

Juan Lopez, foreman of the little ranch of St. Francis in Los Angeles County, one morning in March, 1842, while idly digging up a wild onion, or brodecia, discovered what he thought lumps of gold clinging to its roots. Taking samples of the metal, he rode down to Los Angeles to the office of Don Abel Stearns, who recognized it as gold.

Soon Juan and his companions were busy digging and washing the earth and sands in the region where the little wild flowers grew. These mines were called "placer," from a Spanish word meaning loose or moving about, because the metal was loosely mixed with sand and gravel, generally in the bed of a stream or in a ravine where there had once been a flow of water which had brought the gold down from its home in the mountains.

From these mines Don Abel Stearns sent, in a sailing vessel round Cape Horn, the first parcel of California gold dust ever received at the United States mint, and it proved to be of very good quality.

The San Fernando mines, as they were called, because they were on a ranch that had once belonged to San Fernando mission, yielded many thousand dollars' worth of gold dust. It is on record that one firm in Los Angeles, which handled most of the gold from these and other mines of southern California, paid out in the course of twenty years over two million dollars for southern gold.

The true golden touch, however, was to come in a different part of the territory among people of another race and tongue. It was to transform California from an almost unknown land with slight and scattered population to a community so rich as to disturb the money markets of the world; a community sheltering a great host of people, all young, all striving eagerly for the fortunes they had traveled thousands of miles to find.

After the signing of the treaty of Cahuenga between Colonel Fremont and General Pico, the Spanish-speaking people settled down quietly and peacefully. The only disagreements were between the American leaders, General Kearny and Commodore Stockton, and between Kearny and Fremont, who had been appointed by Stockton military governor of the territory. This appointment General Kearny disputed. General Vallejo tells in one of his letters of having received on the same day communication from Kearny, Stockton, and Fremont, each signing himself commander-in-chief.

Whoever was right in the quarrel, Fremont was the chief sufferer, for General Kearny, after Stockton left, ordered him to return East under arrest and at Washington to undergo a military trial or court-martial for mutiny and disobedience of orders. Although the court found him guilty and sentenced him to be dismissed from the army, the President, remembering his services in the exploration of the West, and quite possibly thinking him not the person most to blame, pardoned and restored him to his position. Fremont, feeling that he had done nothing wrong, refused the pardon and resigned from the army. The next year the new President, Taylor, showed his opinion of the matter by appointing Fremont to conduct the important work of establishing the boundaries between the United States and Mexico.

General Kearny, when he departed for the East, left Colonel Mason, of the regular army, as military governor of California. Mason chose as his adjutant, or secretary, a young lieutenant named Sherman, who, years later, in the Civil War, by his wonderful march through the heart of the South, came to be considered one of the greatest generals of his time.

Soon after the Mexican war many settlers were gathered about Sutter's Fort and San Francisco Bay. There were about two thousand Americans, most of them strong, hardy men, all overjoyed that the territory was in the hands of the United States and all eager to know what would finally be decided in regard to it. Reports kept arriving of parties of emigrants that were about to start overland for California.

"They are as certain to come as that the sun will rise to-morrow," said genial Captain Sutter, "and as the overland trail ends at my rancho, I must be ready to furnish them provisions. They are always hungry when they get there, especially the tired little children, and the only thing for me to do is to build a flour mill to grind my grain."

"Well and good," said James Marshall, one of his assistants, an American by birth, a millwright by trade; "but to build a flour mill requires lumber, and lumber calls for a sawmill."

"We will build it, too," said Sutter. "Take a man and provisions and go up toward the mountains; there must be good places on my land. I leave it all in your hands." The place was found on a swift mountain stream. Near the present site of Coloma, in the midst of pine forests, on the water soon to be so well known as the American River, the sawmill was located. Marshall also marked out a rough wagon road forty-five miles long down to the fort. Captain Sutter was delighted.

"Set to work as soon as you like, Marshall," he exclaimed. "This is your business." Soon the mill was built and almost ready for use.

"You may let the water into the mill race to-night," said Marshall to his men. "I want to test it and also to carry away some of the loose dirt in the bed."

Down came the water with a rush, carrying off before it the loose earth; all night it ran, leaving the race with a clean, smooth bed. The next day, Monday, January 24, 1848,--wonderful day for California--James Marshall went out to look at the mill race to see if everything was ready to begin work.

"To-morrow," thought he, "we will commence sawing, and put things through as fast as possible. The men are waiting, we have plenty of trees down, there is nothing to hinder;" but at that moment as he walked beside the bed of the tail race he saw some glittering yellow particles among its sands. He stopped and picked one up. The golden touch had come.

The following is Marshall's own description as published in the Century Magazine (Vol. 41). "It made my heart thump, for I was certain it was gold. Yet it did not seem to be of the right color; all the gold coin I had seen was of a reddish tinge; this looked more like brass. I recalled to mind all the metals I had seen or heard of, but I could find none that resembled this. Suddenly the idea flashed across my mind that it might be iron pyrites. I trembled to think of it."

Finally, to make sure, Marshall, like Juan Lopez, mounted his horse and rode away to find some one with more knowledge than himself. That some one was Captain Sutter, who looked in his encyclopedia, probably the only one in the territory at that time, and by comparing the weight of the metal with the weight of an equal bulk of water found its specific gravity, which proved it to be gold. Still Sutter thought that he should like better authority. General Sherman, in Memoirs, tells how the news came to Monterey, where, he was the governor's gay young military secretary:--

"I remember one day, in the spring of 1848, that two men, Americans, came into the office and inquired for the Governor. I asked their business, and one answered that they had just come down from Captain Sutter on special business and they wanted to see Governor Mason in person. I took them in to the colonel and left them together. After some time the colonel came to his door and called to me. I went in and my attention was directed to a series of papers unfolded on his table, in which lay about half an ounce of placer gold.

"Mason said tome, 'What is that?' I touched it and examined one or two of the larger pieces and asked, 'Is it gold?' I said that if that were gold it could be easily tested, first by its malleability and next by acids. I took a piece in my teeth and the metallic lustre was perfect. I then called to the clerk, Baden, to bring in an ax and hatchet from the backyard. When these were brought, I took the largest piece and beat it out flat, and beyond doubt it was metal and a pure metal. Still we attached little importance to the fact, for gold was known to exist at San Fernando at the south and yet was not considered of much value."

About this time some of the business men who had settled in the little town of Yerba Buena, finding that all ships that entered the harbor were sent by their owners not to Yerba Buena, of which they knew nothing, but to San Francisco, persuaded the town council to change the name of the settlement from Yerba Buena to San Francisco, which was already the name of the mission and presidio.

"Gold! Gold!! Gold!!! from the American River," cried a horseman from the mines, riding down Market Street, waving his hat in one hand, a bottle of gold dust in the other.

When words like these dropped from the lips of a messenger in any of the little communities, the result was like a powerful explosion. Everybody scattered, not wounded and dying, however, but full of life, ready to endure anything, risk anything, for the sake of finding the precious metal which enables its owner to have for himself and those he loves the comfortable and beautiful things of the world.

The result at San Francisco is thus described in one of its newspapers of 1848: "Stores are closed, places of business vacated, a number of houses tenantless, mechanical labor suspended or given up entirely, nowhere the pleasant hum of industry salutes the ear as of late; but as if a curse had arrested our onward course of enterprise, everything wears a desolate, sombre look. All through the Sundays the little church on the plaza is silent. All through the week the door of the alcalde's office remains locked. As for the shipping, it is left at anchor; first sailors, then officers departing for the mines."

And how was it at the logging camp where Marshall made his great discovery? The new sawmill, built with such high hopes, was soon silent and deserted. No more logs were cut, and no lumber hauled down for the flour mill. There were no men to be found who were willing to cut and saw logs, build mills, or put in the spring wheat when they might be finding their fortunes at the mines.

The newly arrived emigrants suffered no doubt from hunger; maybe the children cried for bread; but most of the men, as soon as they had rested a little and knew what was going on, got together money enough to buy the simple implements of knife, pan, pick, and cradle, which were all the tools necessary for the easy placer mining of those days, and joined the endless procession of those who were pushing up toward the streams and canyons round Sutter's famous sawmill.

As summer came on, the excitement became intense. Not only from the region around San Francisco Bay, but from San Diego and Los Angeles, people came flocking to the mines. Reports were current of men finding hundreds of dollars' worth of gold a day, gaining a fortune in a few weeks. It was almost impossible to hire laborers either in San Francisco or on the ranches. Even the soldiers caught the gold fever and deserted.

In the summer, Governor Mason and Lieutenant Sherman visited the mines. Upon their return to Monterey, having seen for themselves that many even of the wildest rumors were true, they made arrangements to send on to Washington official announcement of the discovery.

How this was accomplished is interesting. A lieutenant of the army was appointed by the governor for the important office, and a can of sample gold was purchased.

The only vessel on the coast ready for departure was a boat bound for Peru. On this ship the lieutenant with his pot of gold and the governor's report embarked at Monterey. He reached the Peruvian port just in time to catch the British steamer back to Panama. Crossing the Isthmus on horseback, he took a steamer for Kingston, Jamaica. There he found a vessel just leaving for New Orleans. Reaching that city he at once telegraphed the news to Washington, trusting it would be in time to form part of the President's message.

On December 5, 1848, the President, in his message to Congress, after speaking of the discovery of gold in California, said, "The accounts of the abundance of gold in that territory are of such extraordinary character as would scarcely command belief but for the authentic reports of officers in the public service who have visited the mineral districts and drew the facts which they detail from personal observation."

The certainty that the wonderful reports of the gold country were true, electrified not only the whole country but the whole civilized world. Large numbers of people began immediate preparation for making the overland journey as soon as the weather should permit; while others, too impatient to wait, left for California by the way of the Isthmus.

In February, 1849, there arrived at Monterey the Panama, the first steamboat to visit the coast. The whole population turned out to see and welcome it. The

Californians as they compared it with the stately frigates and ships they had been accustomed to see, exclaimed, "How ugly!" Although it was not a beautiful vessel, its arrival was an event of great importance, for it was the first of a line of steamers which were under contract to ply monthly between San Francisco and Panama, and with its coming began such an immigration as the world has seldom known.

In 1849 nearly twenty-five thousand people came by land and almost as many more by sea, from the States alone. There were between thirty and forty thousand from other parts of the world.

San Francisco at the time of the discovery had about seven hundred inhabitants, and shortly after only the population of a hamlet, because so many had gone to the gold fields. Now it suddenly found itself called upon to give shelter to thousands of people bound for the mines, and many also returning, some successful, others penniless and eager to get work at the very high wages offered, sometimes as much as thirty dollars a day.

There were streets to be surveyed, houses and warehouses to be built, lumber and brick to be provided. People were living in tents, in brush houses, even in shelter made by four upright green poles over which were spread matting and old bedding. Hundreds of ships lay helpless in the harbor waiting for crews, often for men to unload the cargoes. No longer could the papers complain of lack of business. The town was like a hive, but such a disorderly one as would have driven wild any colony of bees.

All was mud flats or water where are now the water front and some of the leading business streets of the city. On these flats old unseaworthy vessels were drawn up and did duty side by side with rough board buildings as dwellings and stores. In the rainy seasons the streets were lakes of mud where mules and drays were sometimes literally submerged. The arrival of the mail steamer was the event of the month to this host of people so far away from home and loved ones. Guns were fired, bells rang to announce the approach of the vessel, then there was a wild rush to the post office, where the long lines of men, most of them wearing flannel shirts, wide hats, and high boots, extended far down the street. Very high prices were sometimes paid, as high even as one hundred dollars, by a late corner to buy from some one lucky enough to be near the head of the line a position near the delivery window. Then if no letter came, how great was the disappointment!

One man thus described the mines:--

"I was but a lad and my party took me along only because I had a knack at cooking and was willing to do anything in order to see the place where such wonderful fortunes were made. It was a hot summer afternoon when, crossing a region of low, thinly wooded hills, we looked down upon American River; away to the east were high mountain ranges, their peaks, although it was still August, snow-tipped.

"From them came swiftly down the already famous river. Its volume was evidently diminished from the heat, and along its gravelly bed men were digging the sand and gravel into buckets. As I reached them and watched them work I was greatly disappointed. It seemed like very ordinary dirt they were handling; I saw no gleam of the yellow sands of which I had heard such stories. I followed one of the men who carried the buckets of earth to something that looked very like our family cradle with the footboard knocked out. Where the slats might have been there was nailed a piece of sheet iron punched full of holes. Above this was a chute in which the dirt was emptied. The cradle was then rocked violently while water was poured over its contents. The lighter earth and gravel were carried away, while the gold, being heavier, rested either on the sheet iron or between the slats on the cradle bottom.

"Some of the men had no cradle, only a large pan made of sheet iron. This pan, when half filled with dirt, was sunk in the water and shaken sidewise until the dirt and gravel were washed away and only heavy grains of gold remained. There were enough of these to make my eyes open wide. The men who had the cradle were making pretty steadily from eighteen to twenty dollars a day apiece.

"After a day or two I visited the dry diggings. Here I saw things that were more astonishing to me than anything that I had seen at the placer mines. Some men were at work in a little canyon, and I sat on the bowlder and watched them digging into the earth with their knives and picking up every few minutes spoons of earth in which there were plainly visible little lumps of gold the size of a pea. This was considered a rich find; the men were joyful over their success. Suddenly one of the older ones, looking up at me, sang out:--

"Say, Sonny, why do you sit there idle? Out with that bread knife of yours and dig for your fortune. Across this ridge is another ravine. It may be like this. Try your luck, anyway.'

"Somehow, until that moment, it had not entered my boyish mind, that I might join this great mad race for wealth. I sprang to my feet. My heart began to pound faster than it did on the glorious day when in my boyhood home I had won the mile race at the county fair. There was a singing in my ears; for the minute I could scarcely breathe. I had heard of the gold fever, and now I had caught it.

"I dashed up the hillside, fairly rolled down into the rocky little valley beyond, and began to dig wildly; but I found only good honest earth, rich noble soil so like our fertile bottom lands at home. My spirits began to sink, my heart to resume its natural beats. I worked half an hour or so without finding any sign, as it was called, and began to feel discouraged. In the canyon, which was very narrow, a large bowlder blocked my progress. I determined to dig it loose. This was the work of some time, but finally I succeeded in dislodging it, and drawing up my legs out of its way watched with a youngster's delight its wild dash down the mountain side to the stream far below.

"Slowly I turned to resume my work, but what I saw brought me to my feet with a yell. The socket where the stone had rested was dotted with yellow lumps of gold as big as a pea, some even larger. Down I went upon my knees and I fell to work with a will--the strength of a man seemed in my arms. Off came my coat, and spreading it out I scooped the rich dirt into it by the handful. I had happened on a pocket, as it was called; a turn in the bed of some old mountain stream. The dirt from this when washed yielded me about five hundred dollars, but it was all except cook's wages that I ever made at the mines.

"Before I left the gold fields I saw some small attempt at hydraulic mining which later proved so successful. From a stream up in a canyon some enterprising men had built a log flume and connected with it a large hose and nozzle they had brought up from the coast. Turning the water in this on a dry hill rich in gold deposit, they easily and rapidly washed the dirt down into a sluice or trough below. This had bars nailed across, and water running through carried the dirt away while the gold dropped into the crevices between the bars." This method of mining and also quartz mining, that is, digging gold and other metals from rock, is described in another chapter.

The gold-bearing earth extended along the west slope of the Sierra Nevada and their base, from Feather River on the north to the Merced River on the south, a territory about thirty miles wide by two hundred and fifty long. In this district are still some of the richest mines in the world.

Chapter VIII
The Great Stampede

The rush of people to the Pacific coast after the gold discovery may well be called a stampede. The terrible overland journey, over thousands of miles of Indian country, across high mountains and wide stretches of desert, was often undertaken with poor cattle, half the necessary supplies of food, and but little knowledge of the route. On the other hand, those who preferred going by water would embark in any vessel, however unsafe, sailing from Atlantic ports to the Isthmus.

In New York the excitement was especially great. Every old ship that could be overhauled and by means of fresh paint made to look seaworthy was gayly dressed in bunting and advertised to sail by the shortest and safest route to California. The sea trip is thus described by an elderly gentleman who made the journey when a boy of ten:--

"Together with the news of the discovery of gold came also reports of a warm, sunny land which winter never visited, where life could be spent in the open air,--a favorable spot where sickness was almost unknown. It was, I think, as much on account of my mother's health as to make his fortune that my father decided to go to California. The water route was chosen as being easier for her.

"The saying good-by to our relatives had been hard; but by the time we were three miles from home we children ceased to grieve, so interested were we in new sights and experiences.

"I had never seen salt water until that morning in New York, when we boarded the gayly trimmed brig, the Jane Dawson, which was to carry us to the Isthmus. To my sister and myself it was a real grief that our vessel had not a more romantic name. We decided to call it the Sea Slipper, from a favorite story, and the Sea Slipper it has always been to us.

"On the deck there were so many unhappy partings that we became again downhearted, a feeling which was intensified in the choppy seas of the outer bay to the utter misery of mind and body. We got ourselves somehow into our berths, where, with mother for company, we remained for many hours. Finally the sea grew calmer and we were just beginning to enjoy ourselves when off Cape Hatteras a severe storm broke upon us. The vessel pitched and rolled; the baggage and boxes of freight tumbled about, threatening the lives of those who were not kept to their berths by illness.

"Although I was not seasick I dared not go about much. One night, however, growing tired of the misery around me, I crawled over to the end of the farther cabin, which seemed to be deserted. Presently the captain and my father came down the stairs and I heard the officer say in a hoarse whisper. 'I will not deceive you, Mr. Hunt; the mainmast is down, the steering gear useless, the crew is not up to its business, and I fear we cannot weather the night!' I almost screamed aloud in my fright, but just then a long, lanky figure rose from the floor where it had been lying. It was one of the passengers, a typical Yankee.

"'See here, captain,' he said, 'my chum and I are ship carpenters, and the other man of our party is one of the best sailors of the Newfoundland fleet; just give us a chance to help you, and maybe we needn't founder yet awhile.' The chance was given, and we did not founder.

"Some days later we anchored in the harbor of Chagres. There were many vessels in the bay, and a large number of people waiting to secure passage across the Isthmus. They crowded around the landing place of the river canoes and fought and shouted until we children were frightened at the uproar, and taking our hands mother retired to the shade of some trees to wait.

"It was almost night when father called to us to come quickly, as he had a boat engaged for us. It lay at the landing, a long canoe, in one end of which our things were already stored. Some men who were friends of father's and had joined our party stood beside it with revolvers in hand watching to see that no one claimed the canoe or coaxed the boatmen away. Mother and Sue were quickly tucked beneath the awning, the rest of us tumbled in where we could, and at once our six nearly naked negro boatmen pushed out the boat and began working it up the stream by means of long poles which they placed on the bottom of the river bed, thus propelling us along briskly but with what seemed to me great exertion.

"To us children the voyage was most interesting. On either side the banks were covered with such immense trees as we had never dreamed of. The ferns were more like trees than plants, and the colors of leaves and flowers so gorgeous they were dazzling. The fruits were many and delicious, but our father was very careful about our eating, and would not allow us to indulge as we desired.

"The night came on as suddenly as though a great bowl had been turned over us. For an hour or more we watched with delight the brilliant fireflies illuminating all the atmosphere except at the end of the boat, where the red light of a torch lit the scene. After we had lain down for the night the moon rose and I could not enough admire the beauty of the tropical foliage, with the silvery moonlight incrusting every branch and leaf.

"The second day we left the boats and took mules for the rest of the journey. To my delight I was allowed an animal all to myself. Sue rode in a chair strapped to the back of a native, and our luggage was taken in the same manner, the porters carrying such heavy loads that it did not seem possible they could make the journey.

"To my sister and me, the city of Panama was amazingly beautiful, with its pearl oyster shells glittering on steeple and bell tower, and the dress of the people as magnificent as the costumes described in the 'Arabian Nights.' In Panama we waited a long time for a steamer. The town was crowded and many people were ill. My mother was constantly helping some one until my father forbade her to visit any stranger, because cholera had broken out and many were dying.

"It was a joyful morning when we boarded the steamer California, steamed out on the blue Pacific, and headed northward. We had more comfortable quarters and better food than when on the Atlantic; but never on the steamer did we feel the sense of grandeur and power that came to us on the brig when, with white sails all set, she rushed like a bird before the wind.

"Toward the close of the voyage there was so much fog that our captain did not know just whereabouts we were, and for that reason kept well out to sea. One morning there came a rap at the stateroom door, and a loud voice cried, 'Wake up, we shall be in San Francisco in less than an hour.' What a time of bustle followed! The sea was rough. Sue and I fell over each other and the valises in our eagerness to get dressed. I, being a boy, was out first. The sun was shining as though it was making up for the days it was hidden from us. The water was blue and sparkling, the air warm and delightful after the cold, foggy weather.

"We were steaming due east, and almost before I knew it we had passed through Golden Gate and were in the quiet water of the bay. By the time mother and Sue were on deck, we were nearing the wharf. I thought then that San Francisco was rather disappointing in its looks, with its unpainted houses of all kinds of architecture, and the streets like washouts in the hills, but soon I learned to love it with a faithfulness which was felt by many of the pioneers and will end only with life."

Such were some of the hardships and discomforts endured by those who traveled to California by water during the period of the gold excitement. Yet those who made the journey by land often suffered even more.

The first immigrant train to California started in 1841.

It brought among its members a young man named Bidwell, afterward United States representative from California. Describing this journey in the Century Magazine (Vol. 41), Mr. Bidwell says:--

"The party consisted of sixty-nine persons. Each one furnished his own supplies of not less than a barrel of flour, sugar, and other rations in proportion. I doubt whether there was a hundred dollars in money in the whole party, but all were anxious to go.

"Our ignorance of the route was complete. We knew that California lay west, and that was all. Some of the maps consulted and supposed to be correct showed a lake in the vicinity of where we now know Salt Lake to be, that was three or four hundred miles in length, with two outlets, both running into the Pacific Ocean, either apparently larger than the Mississippi River. We were advised to take along tools to make canoes, so that if we found the country too rough for our wagons, we could descend one of these rivers to the Pacific." It was two years later that Fremont, the pathfinder and roadmaker of the West, surveyed the great Salt Lake and made a map of it. The Bidwell party after many hardships reached California in safety.

The unhappy Donner party, also home seekers, made the journey in 1848. They lost their way and became snow-bound in the mountains. A number of them died from cold and starvation, but the remainder were rescued by relief parties sent out from Sutter's Fort. Their sufferings were too terrible to be told, and yet they started with fair hopes and as excellent an outfit as any party that ever crossed the plains. The following is from an account of the journey written by one of their number for the Century Magazine (Vol. 42):--

"I was a child," says Virginia Reed Murphy, "when we started for California, yet I remember the journey well. Our wagons were all made to order, and I can say truthfully that nothing like the Reed family wagon ever started across the plains. The entrance was on the side, and one stepped into a small space like a room, in the center of the wagon. On the right and left were comfortable spring seats, and here was also a little stove whose pipe, which ran through the top of the wagon, was prevented by a circle of tin from setting fire to the canvas. A board about a foot wide extended over the wheels on either side, the full length of the wagon, thus forming the foundation of a large roomy second story on which were placed our beds; under the spring seats were compartments where we stored the many things useful for such a journey. Besides this we had two wagons with provisions.

"The family wagon was drawn by four yoke of choice oxen, the others by three yoke. Then we had saddle horses and cows, and last of all my pony. He was a beauty, and his name was Billy. The chief pleasure to which I looked forward in crossing the plains was to ride on my pony every day. But a day came when I had no pony to ride, for the poor little fellow gave out. He could not endure the hardships of ceaseless travel. When I was forced to part with him, I cried as I sat in the back of the wagon watching him become smaller and smaller as we drove on until I could not see him any more. But this grief did not come to me until I had enjoyed many happy weeks with my pet.

"Never can I forget the morning when we bade farewell to our kindred and friends. My father, with tears in his eyes, tried to smile as one friend after another grasped his hand in a last farewell. My mother was overcome with grief. At last we were all in the wagon, the drivers cracked their whips, the oxen moved slowly forward, the long journey had begun.

"The first Indians we met were the Caws, who kept the ferry and had to take us over the Caw River. I watched them closely, hardly daring to draw my breath, feeling sure that they would sink the boat in the middle of the stream, and very thankful I was when I found that they were not like the Indians in grandmamma's stories.

"When we reached the Blue River, Kansas, the water was so high that the men made rafts of logs twenty-five feet in length, united by cross timbers. Ropes were attached to both ends and by these the rafts were pulled back and forth. The banks of the stream being steep, our heavy-laden wagons had to be let down carefully with ropes so that the wheels might run into the hollow between the logs. This was a dangerous task, for in the wagons were the women and children, who could cross the rapid stream in no other way.

"After striking the great valley of the Platte the road was good, the country beautiful. Stretching out before us as far as the eye could reach was a valley as green as emerald, dotted here and there with flowers of every imaginable color. Here flowed the grand old Platte--a wide, shallow stream. This part of our journey was an ideal pleasure trip. How I enjoyed riding my pony, galloping over the plain gathering wild flowers! At night the young folks would gather about the camp fire chattering merrily, and often a song would be heard or some clever dancer would give us a jig on the hind door of a wagon.

"In the evening, when we rode into camp, our wagons were placed so as to form a circle or corral, into which, after they had been allowed to graze, the cattle were driven to prevent the Indians from stealing them. The camp fire and the tents were placed on the outside of this square. There were many expert riflemen in the party, and we never lacked game. I witnessed many a buffalo hunt and more than once was in the chase close behind my father. For weeks buffalo and antelope steaks were the main article on our bill of fare, and our appetites were a marvel." The Reed family was the only one belonging to the Donner party, it is said, who made the terrible journey without losing a member.

To the young people and men there was often much pleasure in crossing the continent in a prairie schooner, as the white-covered emigrant wagon was called; but to the women it was another matter, since they had to ride constantly in a wagon, attend to the little children, and do the cooking, often under great difficulties. Many of them learned to be experts in camp cooking, requiring nothing more than a little hollow in the hard ground for a range; or if there were plenty of stones, the cooking place might be built up a little. Over this simple contrivance, with the aid of a couple of iron crossbars, a kettle, a frying pan, and coffee pot, many a delicious meal was easily and quickly prepared.

Mrs. Hecox, in the Overland Monthly, says: "I am sure the men never realized how hard a time the women had. Of course the men worked hard too, but after their day's travel was over they sat around the camp fire, smoked, and told stories, while the women were tending the children, mending clothes, and making ready for the next day's meals.

"After we crossed the Mississippi, it commenced raining, and for days we splashed through the mud and slush. When we camped at night, we had to wade about and make some kind of shelter for our fires, and I was obliged to keep the children cooped up in the wagons. Here let me say that I never heard an unkind word spoken among the women all the way across the plain. The children were good, too, and never out of humor either, unless some cross man scolded them.

"At one place a drove of buffalo ran into our train and gave us a bad scare. I was in the wagon behind ours attending a sick woman when I saw the drove coming. I knew the children would be frightened to death without me, so I jumped from the wagon and ran, but I was too late. Finding that I had no time to get into the wagon, I crawled under it, where a wounded buffalo cow tried to follow me. I kicked her in the head as I clung to the coupling pole, and somehow broke my collar bone."

As soon as the grass began to get green in the spring of 1849, after the news of the discovery of gold reached the States, the overland march began. In white-covered emigrant wagons, in carts, on horses, mules, even on foot, came the eager gold seekers. How poorly prepared were many of them, it would be hard to believe. They were a brave and hardy company of people, but they suffered much. It is estimated that at least eight or ten thousand of the young, strong men died before the year was over. Many of these deaths were due to overwork and exposure, to the lack of the necessaries of life at the mines, also to the fact that a great many of the gold seekers were clever, educated people, quite unused to extreme poverty, and therefore lacking in the strength that comes from self-denial.

Those who remained formed the best material for the making of the state. To this class belonged those who endowed the two great universities which are now the glory of California. For many years the highest position in public life was held by men who came to the Golden State over the plains or by the uncomfortable ocean route in the days of '49.

Chapter IX
The Birth of the Golden Baby

The birth of the Golden Baby, in other words, the coming of the Golden State into the Union, was a time of struggle and uncertainty, when feelings were deeply stirred and hope deferred caused bitter disappointment. When the treaty of peace with Mexico was ratified by Congress it left the Pacific coast settlements in a strange position--a territory containing thousands of people, with more coming by hundreds, but with no legally appointed rulers.

As soon as Congress accepted the treaty, the military governor ceased to have any power, for there was then no longer a state of war; yet he was still obeyed by courtesy, until some one with a better right took his place. The only other official was the local alcalde of each community. This was a Mexican office, but was at that time often filled by an American who had, perhaps, been in the territory only a few months and knew nothing of Mexican laws, but ran things as well as he could after the Eastern fashion.

The Rev. Mr. Colton, chaplain of the warship Congress, was made alcalde of Monterey, and his book on those times is most interesting.

"My duties," said he, "are similar to those of the mayor of an Eastern city, but with no such aid of courts as he enjoys. I am supreme in every breach of peace, case of crime, disputed land title, over a space of three hundred miles. Such an absolute disposal of questions affecting property and personal liberty never ought to be confided to one man."

The country owed much to Mr. Colton's work while alcalde. He soon gained the confidence of law-abiding residents, but was a terror to evil doers. Those he put to work quarrying stone and building the solid structure afterward named Colton's Hall. Here one of the first of California's schools was opened, and here was held the first convention.

Perhaps the truth that "as a man sows, so shall he reap," that a wrong action is apt to bring its own punishment, was never more plainly shown than in the Mexican war. The war was brought upon the United States in a great degree by those interested in slavery, not because they had any just cause of quarrel with the people of Mexico, but because they wanted more territory where slaves could be held.

California, which was the name generally given to all the country extending from Mexico northward to Oregon and the Louisiana Purchase, and eastward from the Pacific Ocean to Texas, was what they really fought for, and when they got it, it became their undoing. When a commissioner went to Mexico to arrange for peace, he demanded California for the United States. As is usual, the conquered had to yield to the victor, and Mexico agreed, "provided the United States would promise not to permit slavery in the territory thus acquired."

"No," replied Mr. Trist, the American commissioner, "the bare mention of such a thing is an impossibility. No American president would dare present such a treaty to the Senate."

The Mexican authorities persisted, saying the prospect of the introduction of slavery into a territory gained from them excited the strongest feelings of abhorrence in the hearts of the Mexican people, but the American commissioner made no promise.

In the summer of 1848 the President, in a special message, called the attention of Congress to California and asked that the laws of a territory be granted to it. The South agreed, provided half should be slave territory. The Northern people, who disliked slavery, had no commercial interest in it, and felt it a disgrace to the nation, resisted this demand. Then began a bitter struggle over California and the question of slavery on her soil, which lasted for two years and called forth some of the grandest speeches of those mighty leaders, Webster, Clay, and Calhoun.

In 1849, while this fight in Congress was still going on, an amendment to tax California for revenue, and another which would result in making her a slave state, were added to the regular appropriation bill which provided for the expenses of government and without which the government would stop. Congress was supposed to close its session on Saturday, March 3d, at midnight. The new President, Taylor, was to take office on Monday.

There had been many times of excitement in that Senate chamber, but this night, it is said by those who were present, was equal to any. Such a war of words and a battle of great minds! Many eyes were turned to the clock as it drew near the hour of midnight. Would the stroke of twelve dissolve the meeting and the great government of the United States be left without funds?

To many of the senators this seemed a certainty, but Mr. Webster insisted that Congress could not end while they remained in session. So, through the long night, the struggle went on. About four o'clock the amendment in regard to slavery was withdrawn, and the bill for the government money was passed.

Meantime the American settlers in California were extremely dissatisfied. To be living without suitable laws was an unnatural and dangerous state of affairs which could not be tolerated by men who loved their country and their homes. The Spanish Californians, also, were anxious to know what they had to expect from the laws of the United States. At last it was decided by the people, and agreed to by the military governor, Riley, who was a man of good judgment, that delegates should be chosen to a convention which should arrange a state constitution and government. It was determined, however, to wait for word from Congress, which had closed in such tumult.

News would certainly arrive by the next steamer, the Panama, which was long overdue. It was a favorite amusement in those days for the boys of San Francisco to go upon the hill and watch for her coming. The 4th of June they were rewarded by the sight of her. As she came into harbor a large part of the population hurried to the wharf, eager to learn the action of Congress. Was California to be a state or not?

The disappointment was great when it was found that nothing had been done except to pass the revenue laws, which meant taxation without representation. In the plaza and on the streets the crowds were loud in their disapproval. The excitement was almost as great as in Boston, so long before, when the news of the tax on tea arrived. A mass meeting was called.

"It is plain they expect us to settle the slavery question for ourselves," said one. "We can do it in short order," said another.

Monday, September 3, 1849, the constitutional convention met at Monterey.

"Recognizing the fact that there is need of more than human wisdom, in the work of founding a state under the unprecedented condition of the country," says the minutes of that meeting, "the delegates voted to open the session with prayer." It was decided to begin each morning's work in this way, the Rev. S. H. Willey and Padre Ramirez officiating alternately.

There were present forty-eight delegates, seven of whom were Spanish Californians. Of these Carrillo of the south and General Vallejo of Sonoma were prominent. They were able men, who were used to governing and who understood fairly well the needs of the times. Later, in the United States Senate, Mr. Webster quoted Mr. Carrillo of "San Angeles," as he called it. Another delegate, Dr. Gwin, was a Southern man who had recently come to California for the purpose of gaining the position of United States senator and of so planning things that even though the state should be admitted as free soil, it might later be divided and part be made slave territory.

He depended for this upon the boundaries. If the whole great section was admitted as California, he thought division would surely follow with the southern part for slavery. The people, however, showed themselves opposed to slavery in their new state, and Dr. Gwin soon found that he must either forego his hopes of becoming senator or give way on this point. The constitution finally adopted was that of a free state with its boundaries as they are to-day. The new legislature chose Colonel Fremont and Dr. Gwin senators, and they left in January, 1850, for Washington, taking the new constitution to offer it for the approval of Congress.

While the people of the Pacific coast had been making their constitution, Congress was in session, and the subject of California and slavery was still troubling the nation. The discussion grew so bitter that in January Clay brought forward his famous Omnibus Bill, so called because it was intended to accommodate different people and parties, and contained many measures which he thought would be so satisfactory to the senators that they would pass the whole bill, although part of it provided for the admission of California as a free state.

At once Southerners sprang forward to resist the measure. They realized keenly that slavery could not hold its own if the majority of the country became free soil. They must persist in their demand for more slave territory, or give up their bondmen. Calhoun, the great advocate of slavery, who was at that time ill and near his death, prepared a speech, the last utterance of that brilliant mind, which was delivered March 4th. He was too ill to read it, but sat, gaunt and haggard, with burning eyes, while his friend spoke for him. It closed with the declaration that the admission of California as a slave or a free state was the test which would prove whether the Union should continue to exist or be broken up by secession. If she came in free, then the South could do no less than secede.

Three days later, March 7th, Webster delivered one of the great speeches of his life. In it he said, "The law of nature, physical geography, and the formation of the earth settles forever that slavery cannot exist in California."

Seward followed with a speech mighty in its eloquence. He said: "California, rich and populous, is here asking admission to the Union and finds us debating the dissolution of the Union itself. It seems to me that the perpetual unity of the empire hangs on this day and hour. Try not the temper and fidelity of California, nor will she abide delay. I shall vote for the admission of California directly, without conditions, without qualifications, and without compromise."

On September 9, 1850, California was at last admitted.

From that time the country advanced steadily onward to the terrible period of 1861, when the South put her threat into execution. The Civil War followed, and the abolition of slavery; but from the sorrowful struggle there arose a better and happier nation, a united North and South. There are two things to be remembered: that into the new territory gained from Mexico slavery never entered; and that the wealth which came from the mines of California did much toward strengthening the North in the conflict.

Over half a year the Californians had been waiting for their constitution to be adopted, and for their representatives to be received in Congress. Sometimes it seemed as though the good news would never come.

One October morning word came down from the lookout on Telegraph Hill: "The Oregon is coming in covered with bunting. All her flags are flying." Almost at the same moment throughout the city could be heard the quick booming of her guns as she entered the harbor. With shouts and clapping of hands the people rushed to the wharf. Tears were pouring down the faces of men who did not know what it was to cry; women were sobbing and laughing by turns. The shrill cheers of the California boys rose high above all. There was the report of guns, the cracking of pistols, the joyful pealing of bells. New York papers sold readily at five dollars each. No more business that day. Joy and gayety reigned. At night the city was ablaze with fireworks and mighty bonfires, which the boys kept going until morning.

Messengers started in every direction to carry the news. The way the word came to San Jose was exciting. The new governor, Peter Burnett, was in San Francisco on steamer day. On the very next morning he left for San Jose on the stage coach of Crandall, one of the famous drivers of the West. The stage of a rival line left at the same time. There was great excitement: a race between two six-horse teams, with coaches decorated with flags, and the governor on the box of one of them.

They had to creep through the heavy sands to the mission, but beyond there they struck the hard road, and away they went, horses at a gallop, passengers shouting and singing. As they passed through a town or by a ranch house people ran out, aroused by the hubbub. Off went the hats of all on the coaches.

"California has been admitted to the Union!" some one would shout in his loudest voice, and, looking back, they would see men shaking hands and tossing hats on high, and small boys jigging while shouts and cheers followed them faintly as they disappeared in the distance.

Past San Bruno, San Mateo, Mayfield, they went with a rush, then swept through Santa Clara, then at a gallop down the beautiful Alameda to San Jose, the governor's coach but three minutes in advance of its rival.

A few days later there was the grand ceremony of admission day, which was described in the papers not only of this country but of England as well.

Still, after the rejoicing came a time of anxiety and sorrow. In its treatment of the land question in California the United States made one of the gravest mistakes ever made by a civilized nation.

The man whom the government sent out to investigate the subject, W. C. Jones, was an able Spanish scholar, skilled in Mexican and Spanish law, and his carefully prepared report declared that the greater part of the rancheros had perfect title to their lands, and all that was necessary for the United States to do was to have them resurveyed.

In Congress, Senator Benton and Senator Fremont in most points supported this report as the only just plan. Against the bill that was finally passed Senator Benton protested vigorously, saying that it amounted to confiscation of the land instead of the protection promised by the American government, through Larkin and Sloat.

This law made it necessary for every Californian, no matter how long he had lived on his land, to prove his title to it, and that, too, while the United States attorney resisted his claim inch by inch, as if he were a criminal.

Thus the Spanish American, who was seldom a man of business after the standard of the Eastern states, was forced into the distressing necessity of fighting for what was his own, in courts, the law and language of which he did not understand. Meantime his property was rendered hard to sell, while taxation fell heaviest upon him because he was a large land owner. Often, too, he would have to pay his lawyer in notes, promising to give money when he could get it, and in the end the lawyer often got most of the land which the United States government had left to the unhappy Californian.

The way in which unprincipled men got the better of the rancheros would fill a volume. Guadalupe Vallejo, in the Century Magazine (Vol. 41), tells how a leading American squatter came to her father and said:--

"There is a large piece of your land where the cattle run loose, and your vaqueros are all gone to the mines. I will fence the field at my own expense if you will give me half of it." Vallejo agreed, but when the American had inclosed it, he entered it on the record books as government land and kept it all.

This article also describes the losses of the ranchmen from cattle stealing. It tells how Americans, who were afterward prosperous citizens, were guilty of selling Spanish beef which they knew had been stolen.

The life of the Spanish-speaking people at the mines was made miserable. The American miners seemed to feel that the Californian had no right to be there. Of course there were some of the lower class, many of whom were part Indian, who would lie, steal, or, if they had an opportunity, murder; but often those who were persecuted were not of this type. A woman of refinement, who under the title of "Shirley" wrote her experiences at the mines, says:--

"The people of the Spanish race on Indian Bar, many of whom are highly educated gentlemen, are disposed to bear an ill opinion of our whole nation on account of the rough men here. They think that it is a great characteristic of Columbia's children to be prejudiced, selfish, avaricious, and unjust."

Because in a quarrel a Mexican killed a drunken miner, the men of the Bar determined to drive away all Californians. They captured several, not the guilty one, banished some, and two they sentenced to be flogged. Shirley from her cabin heard what was going on. She tells how one of them, a gentlemanly young Spaniard, begged in vain to be killed rather than be disgraced by whipping. When, finally, he was released, he swore eternal vengeance against the American race.

In San Francisco the disorderly state of affairs caused by the host of criminals gathered there from all over the world, attracted by the discovery of gold, became unendurable. On the city streets robbery and murder were of frequent occurrence, no one was safe, and wrongdoers went unpunished because, frequently, the officers of the law were in league with them. At last the best citizens felt that for the sake of their homes and families they must take matters into their own hands, so they formed an association, seven thousand strong, which was known as the "Vigilantes."

Those who committed crimes were taken by this organization, and, after careful trial, punished. Several of the worst offenders were executed, many were banished from the country, and unjust officials were removed. When law and order were restored, the Vigilantes disbanded.

The example of San Francisco was followed in various parts of the state, especially in the mining camps, where there were many crimes; but not all the Vigilantes displayed the same care and fairness as the people of the larger city, and sometimes terrible mistakes were made, and innocent people suffered.

With thousands of newcomers on the Pacific coast, and the long distance between them and their homes, it was often of the greatest importance to get their parcels and mail to them as promptly as possible. For this reason several express companies were started and did excellent work; but the mail route called the Pony Express was the most interesting. It is well described by W. F. Bailey in the Century Magazine (Vol. 56).

One day in March, 1860, the following advertisement appeared in a St. Louis paper:--

"To San Francisco in eight days. The first carrier of the Pony Express will leave the Missouri River on Tuesday, April 3d, and will run regularly weekly hereafter, carrying letter mail only. Telegraph mail eight days, letters ten days to San Francisco."

From St. Joseph, Missouri, the first start was made. A large crowd was present to see the rider off. The same day, the same hour, the Western mail started on the thousand-mile ride eastward. There would be ten riders each way, with horses changed every twenty-five miles.

Both Sacramento and San Francisco were full of enthusiasm. It was planned to give the first messenger a rousing reception when he should arrive from the East. He was received by crowds as he galloped into Sacramento, and hurried to a swift river steamboat which immediately started for the Bay. News of his coming was telegraphed ahead, and was announced from the stages of the San Francisco theaters so that when he arrived at midnight a large number of people were awaiting him, bands were playing, and bells were ringing; and a long procession escorted him to the company's office.

In all, there were sixty riders of this express company, all young men, light in weight, accomplished riders, coolheaded, and absolutely brave. They were held in high regard by all, and with good reason. Each when he entered the service signed this pledge:--

"I agree not to use profane language, not to get drunk, not to gamble, not to treat animals cruelly, and not to do anything incompatible with the conduct of a gentleman." They also had to swear to be loyal to the Union.

The average journey of one man was seventy-five miles, this to be accomplished in one day, but the men frequently had to double the distance, and once, when the messenger who was waiting was killed by Indians, "Buffalo Bill" (Mr. Cody) made the long trip of three hundred and eighty-four miles, stopping only for meals and to change horses.

By day and by night, through rain and storm, heat and cold, they rode, these brave men, one facing east, the other west, alone, always alone, often chased by Indians, though, owing to their watchfulness and the superiority of their horses, they were seldom caught. A number were, however, killed by immigrants, who mistook them for Indians or robbers.

The great feat of the Pony Express was the delivering of Lincoln's inaugural address in 1861.

With the Southern states claiming to be out of the Union, people were wild to know what the President would say. To St. Joseph, Missouri, the address was hurried. Here it was carefully wrapped in oil skin, consigned to the saddle bags, and amid wild cheers the express was off. Horses were waiting every ten miles. What a ride was that! "Speed, speed! faster, faster!" was the cry. Each man tried to do a trifle better than the last, while the thousands on the Pacific coast seemed to be straining their ears for the sound of the galloping hoof beats which brought nearer to them the brave message of the grand new President. And when the last rider came in, making the final ten miles in thirty-one minutes, what a cheer went up!

One thousand nine hundred and fifty miles in one hundred and eighty-five hours, the message had traveled--at an average of a little more than ten miles an hour--straight across the continent.

When we read of the speed-breaking special trains of to-day, let us not forget what these brave men of the first overland express accomplished in the days of '61.

Chapter X
The Signal Gun and the Steel Trail

Boom! Boom! Boom! Never in history did the firing of a gun have such a powerful effect as that which sent the first shot at the flag of the Union, as it floated over Fort Sumter on that memorable Friday, April 12, 1861.

Fired at a time when most people were hoping for a peaceful outcome of the sectional troubles, it astonished the world and stirred the whole country to its depths.

Across the dry plains and rugged mountains of the West its echoes seemed to roll. The startled people of the Pacific coast looked at each other with anxious, uncertain eyes. No one felt quite sure of his neighbor, and they were so far from the scene of action that the government could not help them. They must settle the great question for themselves. Who was for the Union? Who was against it?

In Washington the President and his advisers waited with keen anxiety to learn what wealthy California would do. Senator Gwin had often spoken in Congress and elsewhere as though it would certainly be one of the states to secede. He and others had talked too, in a confident way, of the "Grand Republic of the Pacific" that might be then formed out of the lands of the Western coast. To lose this rich territory would be a terrible blow to the Union.

From the time of California's admission there had been a constant endeavor on the part of Southern sympathizers to introduce slavery into its territory. A large number of politicians, especially those holding prominent positions, were Southerners, some of whom, like Dr. Gwin, had come to the Pacific coast for the express purpose of winning either the new state or some portion of it for the South and slavery.

They had succeeded in giving it a fugitive slave law that was particularly evil. Under it a colored man or woman could be seized, brought before a magistrate, claimed as a slave, and taken back South without being allowed to testify in his or her own behalf. Neither could a colored person give testimony in a criminal case against one who was white.

Opposed to this strong Southern party one man stood almost alone as the friend of free labor and free soil. This man was David C. Broderick. For years he fought the slavery interests inch by inch in San Francisco, in the state legislature, and finally in the United States Senate.

When he went to Washington he found the same state of affairs as in California--President Buchanan yielding to the Southern demands, Southern members ruling and often terrifying Congress. Broderick at once joined Stephen A. Douglas in the struggle he was then making for free soil in Kansas and the territories, and his speeches were clear and often fierce.

In reply to a speech from a Carolina senator in regard to the disgrace of belonging to the working class, Mr. Broderick said (Congressional Globe, 1857-58), "I represent a state where labor is honorable, where the judge has left his bench, the doctor and lawyer their offices, the clergyman his pulpit, for the purpose of delving in the earth, where no station is so high, no position so great, that its occupant is not proud to boast that he has labored with his own hands. There is no state in the Union, no place on earth, where labor is so honored, so well rewarded, as in California." Mr. Broderick died in the midst of his bright career, murdered in a duel by one of the leading members of the slavery party.

When he died, those of his fellow-citizens who believed much as he did, yet had let him fight secession and slavery lone-handed, recognized what he had done for them--their "brave young senator," as Seward called him, who had kept the evil of slavery from their soil. His work, stopped by the bullet of his enemy, was taken up by the people, and his name became a rallying cry for the lovers of the Union, of honest labor, and of free soil.

News that the war had really begun brought forth the strongest Union sentiments from many of those who had before been careless or indifferent. A mass meeting of the people of San Francisco was held-- business was suspended, flags were flying everywhere, while eager-faced people listened to earnest Union speeches. A few days later the legislature, by an almost unanimous vote, declared in the strongest terms for the Union, offering to give any aid the government might require. No one could longer have any doubt of the loyalty of the state of California.

There were certainly many people from the South who were deeply in sympathy with secession; but these, if honorable men who were able to fight, hurried east to join the Confederate army, or if they chose to remain under the protection of the flag, were generally wise enough to keep their feelings to themselves.

Some there were, however, who, while they enjoyed the law and order of the peaceful state, still spoke, plotted, and schemed for secession. To keep such as these in order it was found necessary to retain most of the California troops in the state for home defense. Those who did reach Eastern battlefields fought well and nobly.

One of San Francisco's ministers was unwise enough frequently to express disloyal views in the pulpit, until one Sunday morning he found the banner he would dishonor floating over his church, and hanging to a post in front of the door a figure intended to represent himself, with his name and the word "traitor" pinned to it. The next day he left for Europe, where he stayed until the close of the war.

Another minister, Thomas Starr King, was one of the most earnest supporters of the government. He organized the California division of the Sanitary Commission for the assistance of sick and wounded soldiers. Chiefly through his influence California gave over a million and a half to that cause, which was one third of the whole expenditure of the Commission.

In 1862 Leland Stanford became governor. He was devoted to the Union, always striving to influence his state to give liberally of its wealth to help the government; and its record in that line was second to none. "A good leader, energetic and long-headed," the governor was called; but no one dreamed that long before he was an old man, he would give for the cause of education in California the mightiest gift ever bestowed by any one man for the benefit of humanity.

During the war, California furnished 16,000 men, two regiments of which were among the best of the Union cavalry. One regiment of infantry was composed of trappers and mountaineers, from whom were taken many "sharpshooters" so famous in assisting the advance of the Northern troops.

In the southern part of the state there was a body of volunteers known as the California Column, also the California Lancers, who, far off though they were, found enough to do. They drove the Southern forces out of Arizona and New Mexico, fought the Apache Indians in several battles, met and defeated the Texas Rangers, and took various military posts in Texas.

Great was the excitement in San Francisco when one morning the United States marshall captured, just as she was leaving the wharf, a schooner fully fitted out as a privateer. She was filled with armed men, and in her cabin was a commission signed by Jefferson Davis in the name of the Confederate States, also a plan for capturing the forts of the harbor, the Panama mail steamer, then en route north, and a treasure steamer soon to, sail for Panama.

In Los Angeles disloyalty was more outspoken and unrebuked by public opinion. Sometimes the surrounding ranchmen, many of whom were in sympathy with the South, on the news of a Southern victory would come into Los Angeles to celebrate with disloyal banners and transparencies. Living on Main Street there was a Yankee, one of the leading citizens, who upon such an occasion would take his rifle and, promenading the flat roof of his wide-spreading adobe, hurl down defiance at the enemy, calling them "rebels" and "traitors" and defying them to come up and fight him man to man. But there must have been a feeling of good fellowship through it all, since no stray bullet was ever sent to put a stop to the taunts of the fiery old Unionist.

Some Spanish soldiers of the California Column, however, grew weary of such open disloyalty, and one night, when off duty, captured two of the Southern ranchmen and proposed to hang them to the oaks in the pasture near where the city of Pasadena now stands. The American officers of the troops, hearing of the affair, hurried out from Los Angeles and begged their men to give up so disorderly and unsoldier-like an idea. "Yes, sirs, it is true, all that you say; but they are rebels, they talk too much; why suffer them to cumber Union ground?" This seemed the only reply they could obtain; but finally the captives were liberated, though advised in the future to guard well their tongues and actions.

The desire for war news from the Eastern states led to the completion of a telegraph line between the Missouri River and San Francisco, and on all sides the need of an overland railroad was also being recognized. Plans for such a road had been frequently presented to Congress, but straightway slavery entered into the question. The South wanted the road, but it must be through Southern territory, while the North favored the middle or northern route; and they could not agree.

On one such occasion Senator Benton spoke in favor of a line that had just been surveyed by Captain Fremont. He was told by those who had other plans that his route was not possible, that only scientific men could lay out a railroad and determine the most practicable ways and easiest passes. But Senator Benton's answer is worth remembering.

"There is," said he, "a class of scientific engineers older than the schools and more unerring than mathematics. They are the wild animals-- the buffalo, elk, deer, antelope, and bear--which traverse the forest, not by compass, but by an instinct which leads them always the right way to the lowest passes in the mountains, the shallowest fords in the rivers, the richest pastures in the forest, the best salt springs, the shortest practicable route between two distant points. They are the first engineers to lay out a road; the Indian follows. Hence the buffalo road becomes the war path. The white hunter follows the same trail in the pursuit of game; after that the buffalo road becomes the wagon road of the emigrant, and, lastly, the railroad of the scientific man."

Through her senators and representatives California spent several years in pushing this matter. In vain they called attention to the fact that the distance from Washington to San Francisco by the way of Cape Horn was 19,000 miles, or more than the entire distance round the earth in the latitude of San Francisco; and that by Panama it was as far as from Washington to Peking in a direct line.

In 1859-60 there appeared in Washington a young engineer named Judah, who had been sent by the people of the Pacific coast to urge the immediate building of the road by the middle route that which was finally chosen. Mr. Judah knew more about the matter than any other man, east or west, and he failed in his mission only because the troubles over slavery and the prospect of immediate secession took up the whole attention of Congress.

However, he came back in no way discouraged, and continued to urge the matter in his cheerful, hopeful way. That he should be hopeful does not seem strange to us who know that the road was built and that it was a great success, but then conditions were different.

"What, build a railroad over those mountains, with their terrible winter snows and landslides, across the desert, where there is absolutely no water? It is impossible, and these men know it; they only want to get the people's money." Such was the type of article one might read at any time in the papers of the day.

Still, Mr. Judah's talk had its results. One June day in 1861, Leland Stanford, a young lawyer, who was at that time Sacramento's chief grocer, Mark Hopkins and Collis P. Huntington, hardware merchants, and Charles Crocker, proprietor of the leading dry-goods store, met and organized the Central Pacific Railroad Company, with Stanford as president, Huntington as vice-president, Hopkins as treasurer, Judah as engineer, and Crocker as one of the directors.

This action seems sensible enough as we write of it, but it was one of the most daring undertakings ever attempted by any body of men. None of the four was rich, all had worked hard for the little they had; but they felt that the country must have the railroad, that without it California could never become a great state. But if they could only push forward, as soon as they had themselves accomplished something, help would come to them from the East and their success would be assured.

Again Mr. Judah went to Washington, and this time he was successful. The war had made the government feel the need of the railway, not only to bind the Pacific coast closer to the eastern half of the continent, but to transport troops to defend its western shores. There were many now ready to vote for the road, and in July, 1862, the bill, having been passed by both houses, was signed by Abraham Lincoln.

It provided for the building of two roads, one from the Missouri River westward, the Union Pacific, and one from the Pacific coast eastward, the Central Pacific, the two to be continued till they met and formed one long line.

On the day that Leland Stanford was inaugurated governor of California, he had the further satisfaction of beginning the construction of the overland railroad by digging and casting the first shovelful of earth. This took place in Sacramento, in the presence of a large gathering of the leading people of the state; and from that time the work went speedily on. It was estimated that the road would cost an average of eighty thousand dollars a mile, though in the mountains the cost was nearer one hundred and fifty thousand.

Not only the right of way, but a large portion of the near-by public lands, were granted by the government to each road, and at the completion of each forty miles of track there was to be further aid. The state of California, the city of San Francisco, and the counties through which the railroad passed, each gave generously to the Central Pacific; but all this did not bring in enough ready money. Huntington in the East and Stanford in the West almost worked miracles in getting funds to begin the work.

In the death of Mr. Judah, which occurred at this time, the company suffered a great loss. Although the enterprise went on to a successful ending, his name dropped out of sight; but those who know, feel that to him California owes a great debt of gratitude. Though she was sure to have the overland sometime, it might have been years later in its accomplishment, but for the faith, energy, and perseverance of Theodore D. Judah.

Charles Crocker now took charge of the building of the road; to accomplish the work he imported Chinese, whom he found peaceable, industrious, and quick to learn. They were arranged in companies moving at the word of command like drilled troops--"Crocker's battalions" they were called. There was need of the greatest haste to get the different portions completed in the time allowed.

"Why," said Crocker, "I used to go up and down that road in my car like a mad bull, stopping along where there was anything wrong, raising Cain with the men that were not up to time."

Neither Mr. Crocker nor Mr. Stanford ever recovered from the strain of that time. It is said that it eventually caused the death of both men.

Meantime the Union Pacific was pushing overland westward as fast as possible. Each road was aiming for the rich plains of Utah. If the Central stopped at the eastern base of the mountains, it would make this road of little value except for Pacific coast traffic; but if it could reach Ogden, the line would pay well.

It was a mighty race all through the winter of 1868 and 1869, Crocker and his men working like giants. What he accomplished then was scarcely less wonderful than Napoleon's passage of the Alps.

All the supplies for his thousands of workmen, all the materials and iron for the road, even the locomotives, he had to have hauled on sledges over the mountains through the winter snows.

Ogden was finally made the place where the two roads joined; but they first met, and the last work was done, at Promontory, a point fifty miles northwest of

Ogden. There in May, 1869, the last tie was laid. It was made of California laurel, handsomely polished, and on it was a silver plate with an inscription and the names of the officers of the two roads.

It was an eventful meeting on that grassy plain, under the blue Western sky, while all around rose the rugged peaks that had at last been conquered by man's energy. The telegraph at this spot was, for the occasion, connected with all the offices along the line and in the leading cities of the country, where crowds were in waiting to hear that the great work was finished.

Two trains were there with their engines, as Bret Harte describes them, "facing on the single track, half a world behind each back." Around stood the guests and officers of the roads waiting for the final ceremony. "Hats off," clicked the telegraph. Prayer was offered, and then the four gold and silver spikes, presented by California, Nevada, Idaho, and Montana, were put in place by President Stanford of the Central Pacific and Dr. Durant of the Union Pacific.

As the silver hammers fell on the golden spikes, in all the telegraph offices along the line and in the Eastern cities the hammer of the magnet struck the bell-- "tap, tap, tap." "Done,"--flashed the message to the eager crowds.

All over the land the event was celebrated with great rejoicing. In Buffalo, as the news came, hundreds of voices burst out in the singing of "The Star-Spangled Banner." In Boston, services were held at midday in Trinity Church, where the popular pastor offered "thanks to God for the completion of the greatest work ever undertaken by men."

To the four men who were the builders of the Central Pacific, the public and particularly the state of California owes much. They not only built the road, but made it a grand, complete success in all its departments. Without it, California would still be a remote province, little known. With it she is one of the chief states of the Union, and in the great business world she is known and felt as a power.

Later the corporation became very wealthy and powerful. Then it was that it began to abuse its power, working often against the best interests of the inhabitants of the Pacific slope. In some cases, as in the eviction of the people who were settlers in the Mussel Slough District, it was guilty of extreme cruelty and injustice, such as is almost certain to bring its own punishment. But in reckoning with the Southern Pacific, for so the company is now called, the people of California should be careful to look on both sides of the question, remembering the terrible struggles of those early days, when the building of the Overland, that greatest achievement America had ever seen, was to them like the miraculous gift of some fairy godmother, seemingly beyond the possibility of nature.

Chapter XI
That Which Followed After

About the time that the people of California were beginning to feel the trouble arising from the unlimited wealth and power of the great railroad corporation, they discovered what they felt was danger coming from another quarter. This was in the large number of Chinese pouring into the state. Already every town of importance had its quaint Chinese quarter, bits of Asia transplanted to the western hemisphere. Yet these sons of Asia, with their quiet, gliding motions and oriental dress, had been of great service in the development of the new land. Many of the most helpful improvements were rendered possible by their labor, and for years they were almost the only servants for house or laundry work to be obtained. Never did the housewives of the Pacific coast join in the outcry against the Chinese.

Although all this was true, it was also a fact that an American workingman could not live and support his family on the wages a Chinaman would take; and when the white man saw the Chinese given the jobs because they could work cheaply, he became discouraged and angry. Was he to be denied a living in his own country because of these strangers? For this reason the working people became very bitter toward the Chinese.

Their complaints were carried to Washington, and because of them the government finally arranged with China for the restriction of immigration, but not, however, before the matter caused much trouble in California.

During the years 1876-77 times were rightly called "hard" along the Pacific slope. Often laboring men could not get work, and their families suffered. The blame for all this was unjustly given to the Chinese, who were several times badly treated by mobs. The general discontent led at last to a demand for a new state constitution, which many people thought would remedy the evils of which they complained.

For twenty-five years the old constitution had done good service. On the day it had been signed, Walter Colton, alcalde of Monterey, wrote thus of it in his diary: "It is thoroughly democratic; its basis, political and social equality, is the creed of the thousands who run the plow, wield the plane, the hammer, the trowel, the spade." Still it had its faults, the greatest of which was the power given the legislature over public moneys and lands, as well as the chance it allowed for dishonesty in voting.

Unfortunately many of the delegates to the convention which was to make the new constitution were foreigners who knew very little of American manners, customs, and laws, and few of them were among the deeper thinkers of the state, men who had had experience in lawmaking. That the new constitution is not much better than the old, many who helped in the making of it will agree. It was adopted in May, 1879. Since that time it has received a number of changes by means of amendments voted for by the people, and in spite of whatever errors it has contained, the state under it has gone forward to a high degree of prosperity.

In 1875, during the administration of Governor Pacheco, the first native state governor, an invitation was extended to native-born boys of San Francisco to take part in the Fourth of July celebration. A fine body of young men were thus assembled, of whom Hittell in his story of San Francisco says, "They were unparalleled in physical development and mental vigor, and unsurpassed in pride and enthusiasm for the land that gave them birth." This gathering led to the founding of the "Native Sons of the Golden West," an organization which now numbers many thousands and of which the great state may well be proud. Later there was organized a sister society of native daughters, and this also has a large membership. As stated in their constitution, one of the main objects of these sons and daughters of the West is "to awaken and strengthen patriotism and keep alive and glowing the sacred love of California."

An event of the utmost importance to the southern part of the state was the completion of the railroad between San Francisco and Los Angeles, which occurred in 1879. Its route lay through the rich valley of the San Joaquin. Work had been carried on from each end of the line, and it was a very happy assembly which gathered to witness the junction of the two divisions, the event taking place at the eastern end of the San Fernando tunnel. This road was afterward extended from Los Angeles eastward by the way of Yuma and Tucson, and is to-day the Southern Pacific

Overland. Later the Santa Fe Company built its popular road between Los Angeles and the Eastern states. Both these companies now have lines from Los Angeles to San Diego, and the Southern Pacific has a coast road the length of the state, along which the scenery is of great beauty.

Indians

In the history of the state the most pathetic portion is that which relates to the Indians. Bancroft says, "The California valley cannot grace her annals with a single Indian war bordering upon respectability. It can boast, however, a hundred or two of as brutal butcherings on the part of our honest miners and brave pioneers as any area of equal extent in our republic." Miners and settlers coming into the country would take up the waters where the natives fished, the land where they hunted, driving them back to rocky soil, where there was nothing but acorns and roots to support life. As a result the poor, unhappy creatures, driven by hunger, would steal the newcomers' horses and cattle. It is true that the white men depended, in a great measure, upon their animals for the support of their families; but they thought only of their own wrongs, and would arm in strong parties, chase the wretched natives to their homes, and tear down their miserable villages, killing the innocent and guilty alike. The government was the most to blame, because it did not in the first place enact laws for the protection of the Indians in their rights.

About the towns, many of the natives gathered for work. In some places the authorities had the right to arrest them as vagabonds and hire them out as bondmen to the highest bidder, for a period often of as many as two or three months at a time, with no regard to family ties. Little seems to have been done to assist them to a better kind of life. In Los Angeles, when working in the vineyards as grape pickers, they were paid their wages each Saturday night, and immediately they were tempted on all sides by sellers of bad whisky and were really hurried into drunkenness. Their shrieks and howls would, for a time, make the night hideous, when they were driven by the officers of the law into corrals, like so many pigs or cattle, and left there till Monday morning, when they were handed over to whoever chose to pay the officers for the right to own them for the next week.

Near the Oregon line lived some of the most warlike and troublesome Indians of California. Here there were one or two severe fights, the worst of which was with the Modocs, in the northern lava beds. It was here that General Canby was killed.

To-day the Modocs are still suffering keenly. In the upper part of the state the Indians have no lands of any kind, and noble men and women of California are working to secure for them their rights from the government. In the south, whole villages have been found living on nothing but ground acorn meal, from which miserable diet many children die and older people cannot long sustain life.

The Sequoya League, an association for the betterment of the Indians of the Southwest, has done much toward opening the eyes of the public and of the government officials to the unhappy condition of these first owners of the soil. Congress, in 1906, appropriated $100,000 to be used in buying land and water for those Indian reservations or settlements where the suffering was greatest. This was a good beginning, but as the needy Indians are scattered all over the state, much more is required before they can be so placed that they can earn a living by their labors.

Sheep Industry

Gradually the cattle industry, which was for so long a time the leading business of the country, gave way to sheep raising. During summer and fall large flocks of grayish white merinos could be seen getting a rich living on the brown grasses, the yellow stubble of old grain fields, and the tightly rolled nuts of the bur clover; while in winter and spring, hills and plains with their velvet-like covering of green alfileria offered the best and juiciest of food. This was the time of the coming of the lambs. As soon as they were old enough to be separated from their mothers they were put during the day in companies by themselves. A band of five or six hundred young lambs, playing and skipping over the young green grass they were just learning to eat, was a beautiful sight to everybody save to the man or boy who had them to herd. They led him such a chase that by the time he had them safely corralled for the night, every muscle in his body would be aching with fatigue.

Shearing time was the liveliest portion of the herder's life, which was generally very lonely. First came the shearing crew with their captain; next arrived the venders of hot coffee, tamales, tortillas, and other Mexican dainties; brush booths were erected and a brisk trade began. The herds were driven up and into a corral where several shearers could work at a time. Snip, snip, snip, went the shears hour after hour. It was the boast of a good shearer that he could clip a sheep in seven minutes and not once bring blood. As fast as cut, the wool was packed in a long sack suspended from a framework. The dust was dreadful, and the man or boy whose duty it was, when the bag was partly full, to jump in and tramp the wool down so that the bag might hold more, would nearly choke before he emerged into the clear daylight.

The passage of the no-fence law by the legislature of 1873, while it was opposed by the sheep and cattle men, was one of the greatest aids to the growth of agriculture, especially in the southern part of the state. It provided that cattle and sheep should not be allowed to run loose without a herder to keep them from trespassing. This saved the farmer from the necessity of fencing his grain fields, a most important help in a country where fence material was so scarce and expensive.

Colony Days

For some time after California's admission to the Union most of the events of importance in its history took place around the Bay of San Francisco and the junction of the Sacramento and San Joaquin; but early in the seventies the south land awoke from its long sleep and took part in history making, not in such stirring incidents as those of the days of '49, but in a quieter growth that was yet of importance in the making of the state. People in the East had begun to find out that southern California had a mild, healthful climate and that, though the sands of her rivers and rocks of her mountains were not of gold, still her oranges, by aid of irrigation, could be turned into a golden harvest, and that all her soil needed was water in order to yield most bountiful crops.

As little land could be bought in small ranches, those wishing to settle in the country chose the colony plan. A number of families would contribute to a common sum, with which would be purchased a large piece of land of several thousand acres with its water right. Each man received from this a number of acres in proportion to the amount of money he had invested. The first colony formed was that of Anaheim; then followed Westminster, Riverside, Pasadena, and many others, and by that time people began to come into southern California in large numbers.

The overland journey was much longer, then than now, but quite as pleasant. At twenty-two miles an hour the country could be seen and enjoyed, acquaintance made with the plump little prairie dogs of the Nebraska plains, and their neighbors the ground owls, which bobbed grave salutes as the train passed by. Bands of galloping deer, groups of grave Indian warriors sitting on their ponies watching the train from afar, an occasional buffalo lumbering along, shaking his shaggy head, were the things that interested the traveler who took the overland trains in '74 and '75.

At that time between San Francisco and Los Angeles there were two forms of travel: a hundred miles of railroad, with the rest of the distance by stage; and the steamship line. Families chose the ship. From San Pedro to Los Angeles was the only railroad of the southern country. In Los Angeles the flat-roofed adobe buildings, where people could walk about on the tops of the houses, were a wonder to the Eastern strangers. Beautiful homes some of them were, where glimpses could be had of stately senoras in silks and laces, and beautiful senoritas whose dark eyes made havoc with the hearts of the colony young men. The young Californian, who seemed a very part of his fiery steed, was at once the admiration and envy of the Yankee boy.

Queer sights were to be seen at every turn. Creaking carretas, whose squeaking wheels announced their coming a block away, filled the streets, some loaded with grapes, others with rounded shaggy grease-wood roots or sacks of the red Spanish bean and great branches of flaming red peppers. The oxen, with yoke on the horns, seemed as if out of some Bible picture.

Life in the different colonies was much the same. The newcomers had many things to learn, but they made the best of their mistakes, and days of hard work, such as many of them had never known, were often ended with social or literary meetings, where minds were brightened and hearts warmed by friendly intercourse.

When the rains were heavy, the swift mountain streams could not be crossed, and often provisions gave out; then with neighborly kindness those who had, loaned to those who had not, until fresh supplies could be obtained. To this day the smell of new redwood lumber, the scent of burning grease-wood brush, will bring back those times to the colonists with a painful longing for the happy days of their new life in the new land. Many never gained wealth, while some lost lands and savings; but it was these earnest, intelligent men and women who developed the rich valleys of the south land and to whom we are indebted for the bloom and beauty found there to-day.

The result of the land laws and the ill-treatment of the Mexican population at the mines was a period of highway robbery by bands of outlaws, each under the leadership of some especially daring man. The story of some of their adventures reminds the hearer of the tales of Robin Hood. Not so mild as Robin's were their lives, however. Often their passage was marked by a trail of blood, where bitter revenge was taken because of bitter wrongs. Last of these bands was that of Vasquez, who robbed the colony folk gently with many apologies. He was finally captured and executed, and with him the bandits passed from the page of state history.

Alaska

One night in 1867 there took place in Washington an event that was to be of great importance to the western part of the United States. This was the signing of the treaty for the purchase of Alaska. As early as 1860 Mr. Seward, in a speech delivered at St. Paul, said:

"Looking far off into the northwest I see the Russian as he occupies himself establishing seaports, towns, and fortifications, on the verge of this continent, and I say, 'Go on and build up your posts all along the coast up even to the Arctic Ocean, they will yet become the outposts of my own country.'" So long ago did the desire for Alaska, or Russian America as it was then called, possess the mind of the great statesman. But it was not until seven years later that he found the chance to win the government to his views. One evening, while the matter was under discussion between the two countries, the Russian minister called upon Mr. Seward at his home, to inform him that he had just received the Czar's sanction for the sale.

"Good, we will sign the treaty to-night," said the American statesman.

"What, so late as this, and your department closed, your clerks scattered?" remonstrated the Russian.

"It can be done," replied Mr. Seward; and it was. At midnight the treaty was signed. The price paid for Alaska was less than the cost of two of our modern battleships. Every year has proved more and more the wisdom of the purchase. The discovery of gold in particular has immensely increased its value and has brought to California an enlarged commerce.

Spanish-American War

In 1898 came the war with Spain. The tidings of the 15th of February, 1898, filled the hearts of the people of California with indignation and grief. That the United States battleship Maine had been blown up in Havana harbor and numbers of our seamen killed, seemed to many sufficient cause for immediate war. Some, however, feared for the Pacific coast settlements, with insufficient fortifications and no war vessels of importance, except the magnificent Western-built battleship,

Oregon. This vessel was at Puget Sound when the news of the blowing up of the Maine reached her. At the same time came orders to hurry on coal and proceed to San Francisco. There ten days were spent in taking on as much coal and provisions as the vessel could carry. Then, with orders to join the Atlantic fleet as quickly as possible, on the morning of March 19 she steamed through Golden Gate and turned southward, to begin one of the longest voyages ever made by a battleship.

The people of California were sad at heart to part with their noble vessel, and when, in April, war was declared, thousands followed the loved ship and her brave men with their interest and prayers. All alone upon the great sea she was sailing steadily onward, to meet, perhaps, a fleet of foes, or worse still, a dart from that terror of the waters, a torpedo boat; yet always watchful and always ready for whatever foe might appear, she journeyed on.

The order given by Captain Clark to his officers in case they sighted the Spanish squadron, was to turn and run away. As the Spanish ships followed they were almost sure to become separated, some sailing faster than others. The Oregon having a heavy stern battery, could do effective fighting as she sailed; and if the enemy's ships came up one at a time, there might be a chance of damaging one before the next arrived.

Through two oceans and three zones, fifteen thousand miles without mishap, the Oregon sailed in fifty-nine days. When she joined the fleet where it lay off Cuba, she came sweeping in at fifteen knots an hour, the winner of the mightiest race ever run, cheered at the finish by every man of the American squadron. All honor should be given to her wise captain and brave crew and to the Western workmen who made her so stanch and true.

On a fair May day, while California children were rejoicing over their baskets of sweet May flowers, the first battle of the war was fought, the first, and for California the most important. When Dewey destroyed the Spanish fleet on that Sunday morning (May 1, 1898) in Manila Bay, he not only won an important victory, but a greater result lay in the change of attitude of the United States toward the rest of the world.

It was a change which had begun long before; many events had led up to it, but possession of the Philippines and other islands of the Pacific forced our country to recognize the importance of Asia and the ocean which washes its shores.

Commerce has always moved westward, going from Asia to Greece, to Rome, to western Europe, to the western hemisphere; and the race which takes up the movement and carries it forward is the one which gains the profits. All must realize the truth of Mr. Seward's prophecy when he said, "The Pacific coast will be the mover in developing a commerce to which that of the Atlantic Ocean will be only a fraction." "The opportunity of the Pacific," some one has called it. Nearly two thirds of the people of the earth inhabit the lands washed by the waters of this western sea, and the country which secures their trade will become the leading nation of the world--a leadership which should be of the best kind, supplying the needs of peaceful life, building railroads, encouraging the things that help a people upward and onward. To the young men of California, Hawaii and the Philippines offer every chance for daring, energy, and invention. If to honesty and energy there be added a speaking knowledge of the Spanish language, there lie before the youth of the Pacific coast the finest opportunities for active, successful lives.

As soon as President McKinley issued his call to arms for the Spanish war, the men of California responded with a rush. A large number of those who had enlisted were hurried to San Francisco, where the military authorities were quite unprepared to furnish supplies. For a day or two there was real suffering; then the Society of the Red Cross came to the rescue, and thousands of dollars' worth of food and blankets were sent to the camp. As soon as the always generous people of San Francisco comprehended the state of affairs, there was danger that the hungry young soldiers would be ill from overfeeding.

The twenty-third day of May, 1898, is a day to be remembered in the history of our country, for on that day went out the first home regiment from the mainland of the United States, to fight a foe beyond the sea. When the twelve companies of California Volunteers marched through the city from the Presidio to the docks of the Pacific Mail and Steamship Company, two hundred thousand people accompanied them. So hard was it for our peace-loving people to understand the real meaning of war that it was not until the brave lads and earnest men were actually marching to the steamer which was to carry them thousands of miles to meet danger and death, that many quite realized the sorrowful fact. Men cheered the regiment as it passed, but the sobs of the women sometimes nearly drowned the hurrahs. Said one officer, "It was heartrending. If we had let ourselves go, we would have cried our way to the dock." But in the war the record of the California troops was one that gave new honor to their state.

Annexation of Hawaii

"The Hawaiian Islands," said Walt Whitman, in the Overland Monthly, "are not a group. They are a string of rare and precious pearls in the sapphire center of the great American seas. Some day we shall gather up the pretty string of pearls and throw it merrily about the neck of the beautiful woman who has her handsome head on the outside of the big American Dollar, and they will be called the beautiful American Islands."

In 1893 the native queen of the islands was deposed by a revolution conducted in a great measure by Americans living in Hawaii. A provisional government was formed and an application made for annexation to the United States. Through two presidential terms the matter was discussed both in Congress and by the people all over the country. Many were against extending our possessions beyond the mainland in any direction. Others thought it unfair to the natives of the islands to take their lands against their will. It seemed to be pretty well proved, however, that the native government was not for the advancement and best interests of the country, and that in a short time these kindly, gentle people would have to give up their valuable possessions to some stronger power.

Captain Mahan, writing of these conditions, said: "These islands are the key to the Pacific. For a foreign nation to hold them would mean that our Pacific ports and our Pacific commerce would be at the mercy of that nation."

In the early part of the Spanish war (July, 1898) the resolution for the annexation of the Hawaiian Islands was passed by Congress and approved by President McKinley, and the string of pearls was cast about Columbia's fair neck.

Pius Fund

It seems strange that the first case to be tried in the peace court of the nations at the Hague should have been in regard to the Pius Fund of the Californias collected by the Jesuit padres two hundred and thirty years before, to build missions for the Indians of California. The way in which this money was obtained is described in Chapter IV of this history. It grew to be a large sum, of which the Mexican government took control, paying the interest to the Roman Catholic Church in Upper and Lower California. After the Mexican war, Mexico refused to pay its share to the

Church of Upper California. The United States took up the matter, claiming that according to the treaty which closed the war, the Catholic Church of the state of California had a right to its Mexican property.

In 1868 it was agreed by the two countries to leave the matter to the decision of Sir Edward Thornton, English ambassador at Washington. He decided that Mexico should pay an amount equal to one half the interest since the war. Mexico did this, but had paid nothing during all the years which had passed since that time. To settle the dispute finally, it was decided to leave it to arbitration by the Hague court. The verdict given was that Mexico should pay the Roman Catholic Church of California $1,400,000 for the past, and one half the interest on the fund each year from February, 1903, forever.

Panama Canal

The natural result of the nation's need in the Civil War was the overland railroad. The danger to the Oregon on its long journey, the difficulties in getting reinforcements to Admiral Dewey, and the possession of new lands in the Pacific led to decided action in regard to the building of a ship canal through the Isthmus of Panama.

For years the plan had been talked over. In General Grant's first term as President he saw so plainly our need of this water way, that he arranged a canal treaty with Colombia, and it seemed as though the work would soon begin, but the Colombian government refused to allow the matter to go on, hoping to make better terms with the United States. This was not possible then, so the plan was not carried out. Later, a French company undertook to build a canal across Panama, but after several years of work failed.

Many of the Americans favored the route through Nicaragua, but after the government had spent much money and time in considering carefully both propositions, the preference was given to the Panama route. In 1902 an act for the building of the canal was passed by Congress and approved by President Roosevelt. It provided, however, that should the President be unable to obtain a satisfactory title to the French company's work and the necessary territory from the republic of Colombia on reasonable terms and in a reasonable time, he should seek to secure the Nicaragua route. The matter was almost settled, when again Colombia's greed got the better of her judgment and she refused to ratify the compact.

When the people of the province of Panama saw that they were likely to lose their canal through the action of their government, they promptly revolted and declared themselves independent of Colombia. The United States recognized their independence, and a satisfactory treaty was at once concluded with them. In March, 1904, the commission appointed by the President for building the canal sailed for the Isthmus.

Nearly one fourth of the work had already been done by the old company, but there was yet a great deal to do. Besides the actual building of the canal, its dams and locks, the fever district had to be made healthful enough for workmen to live there, marshes had to be drained, pure water brought in from the mountains, and the fever-spreading mosquitoes killed. In addition to all this, the natives of the land and the many bands of workmen of different races had to be brought into an orderly, law-abiding condition. In less than a year it was found necessary to alter the commission, the President choosing this time men particularly noted for their energy and power to make things go. The work progressed with great rapidity, until, in August, 1914, the canal was opened to navigation.

The Orient

In the latter part of the nineteenth century the eastern portion of Asia began to stir itself, rising up from the sleepy, shut-in life it had led for hundreds of years. The eyes of the world watched in wonder the progress of the war between China and Japan (1894-95). In it was fought the first battle in which modern war vessels were engaged. It was found that the Japanese, of whom so little was then known, could fight, and fight well.

As a result of the war, China ceded to Japan the territory of Manchuria and the right to protect Korea. Russia and Germany objected, however, and France agreed with them, so Japan had to give way. Soon Russia began taking possession of the disputed territories, but she had constant trouble with Japan, and early in 1904 war broke out. Before the close of the year the civilized world stood astonished not only at the wisdom, patriotism, and fighting qualities of the Japanese, but also at their humanity, which would not have discredited a Christian nation.

There took place a series of great battles, both on land and on the sea, in which the Japanese were generally victorious. The terrible loss of life and destruction of property led the President of the United States, in the spring of 1905, to urge upon the two countries that fighting cease and peace be arranged.

Few statesmen believed that Mr. Roosevelt would be successful in his humane endeavor, but he pushed his suggestion with patient perseverance until, in September, 1905, Americans had the satisfaction of witnessing upon their soil, at Portsmouth, New Hampshire, the signing of the treaty of peace between Russia and Japan.

Japan's methods of conducting the war had advanced her to a standing among nations which she had never before occupied, and all realized the wisdom of securing commercial relations with her people, who were so rapidly adopting the habits and customs of the rest of the civilized world. In this competition for her commerce, California, by her position on the western shore of the United States, has unusual advantages, a fact which was soon proved by the amount of money invested in increasing her facilities for production and manufacturing. Unfortunately little has yet been done in the matter of shipbuilding, and few vessels which enter her harbors have been built in the state.

Some Recent Events

"I'll put a girdle around the earth in forty minutes," prophesied Puck in "Midsummer Night's Dream." The boastful fairy did not succeed in accomplishing this wonder until midnight on the Fourth of July, 1903. On that day the Pacific cable from the United States to Hawaii, to Midway Island, to Guam, and to Manila, began operations. The men worked hard that last day of the cable laying, and by 11 P.M. the President of the United States sent a message to Governor Taft at Manila. Soon after was the old prophecy fulfilled, when President Roosevelt, no doubt with Puck at his elbow, sent a message round the world in twenty minutes, thus bettering Puck's idea by half.

The saddest year in California's records is that of 1906. On the morning of April 18, a great and overwhelming calamity overtook the beautiful region around San Francisco Bay. A movement of the earth's crust which began in the bottom of the ocean far out from land, reached the coast in the vicinity of Tomales Bay in Marin County. Wrecking everything that came in its direct path, it shivered its way in a southeasterly direction to a point somewhere in the northern part of Monterey County. The land on the two sides of the fault moved a short distance in opposite directions. Thus in some straight fences and roads crossing the fault, one section was found to be shifted as much as sixteen feet to one side of the other. The severe vibrations set up by this break and shifting extended a long distance in all directions.

Although the earthquake was by no means so severe in San Francisco as in the region of Tomales Bay or even in the vicinity of Stanford, Santa Rosa, San Jose, or Agnews, it caused greater loss of life and property on account of the crowded population. Many buildings were wrecked, especially those poorly constructed on land reclaimed from swampy soil or built up by filling in.

People who had prophesied that, should an earthquake come, the high buildings such as those of the Call and the Chronicle would surely collapse, were astonished to see those giant structures apparently unharmed while buildings of much less height, but without the steel framework, were completely wrecked.

The earthquake was a sad calamity, but had this been the sum of the disaster the city would only have paused in its progress long enough to clear away the wreck and to sorrow with the mourners. It was the fires which sprang up while the water system was too damaged to be of use that wiped out old historical San Francisco, leaving in its place a waste of gray ashes and desolate ruins. Santa Rosa, San Jose, Stanford, Agnews, all suffered severely from the earthquake; but in few cases did fires arise to add to their loss. The State Insane Asylum at Agnews, which was built on swampy ground, was a complete wreck with large loss of life.

The marvelous bravery and cheerfulness with which the people of San Francisco bore their cruel fate gave a lesson in courage and unselfishness to humanity. The magnificent generosity with which not only the people of southern and northern California, but of the whole country, sprang to the relief of the unhappy city gave a silver lining to the black cloud of disaster.

Before the embers of their ruined homes had ceased to smoke the people began the work of rebuilding, and at the time of the visit of the Atlantic fleet of the United States navy in 1908, business had so revived as to be almost normal, and the welcome accorded the silent vessels in white by the gallant City of St. Francis was as hearty and generous as any that greeted them during their progress.

October, 1909, was marked by two events of importance to San Francisco. One was the visit of President Taft, to whom the great state of California had given all its electoral votes. The second was the celebration, at the same time, of the discovery of the bay, which occurred in the fall of 1769, the founding of the presidio and mission, which took place in the fall of 1776, and the rebuilding of the burned district. On this occasion the people of San Francisco and their guests gave themselves up to a time of merrymaking--a three days' historical carnival called, in honor of the commander of the expedition during which the great bay was discovered, the "Portola Festival."

In 1915 the Panama-Pacific International Exposition was held in San Francisco. It contained many novel and beautiful features, and was attended by vast multitudes of people. Another notable exposition was held at San Diego, beginning in 1915 and continuing in 1916.

Chapter XII
"The Groves Were God's First Temples"

If the people of this century continue the destruction of trees as they are doing at present, a hundred years from now this will be a world without forests, a woodless, treeless waste. What a desolate picture is this! What a grave charge will the people of the future have to bring against us that we recklessly destroy the trees, one of God's most beautiful and useful gifts to man, without even an endeavor to replace the loss by replanting!

During the last hundred years the American lumber belt has moved westward over a wide space. In the early days of our history nearly the entire supply came from Maine, and what interesting stories we have of those brave pioneer loggers and settlers! Gradually the noble woods which furnished the tall, smooth masts for which American ships were famous, were destroyed; and the ringing ax blows were then heard in the forests about the Great Lakes and in the middle Southern states. This supply is by no means exhausted, but to-day the heart of the lumber interest is on the Pacific coast.

Around the great central valley which is drained by the Sacramento and the San Joaquin rivers, six hundred and forty miles long, lie mountain ranges on whose slopes are some of the noblest forests of the world. To the north of the central valley the trees of the east and west join, forming a heavily wooded belt quite across the state.

In the trade, the greatest demand is for lumber of the pine and fir trees, and of these California has as many species as Europe and Asia combined. She has, indeed, only a little less than one fifth of all the lumber supply of the United States. Her most valuable tree for commerce is the sugar pine. It attains a diameter of twelve feet or more and is often two hundred feet high. But the most interesting trees of California and of the world are the Sequoias, the oldest of all living things. Very far back, in the time of which we have no written history, in the moist days of gigantic vegetation and animals, the Sequoias covered a large portion of the earth's surface; then came the great ice overflow, and when that melted away, almost the only things living of the days of giants were the Sequoias of middle and upper California, and those on some two thousand acres over the Oregon line.

The Sequoia sempervirens, which is commonly called redwood, is distributed along the Coast Range, the trees thriving only when they are constantly swept by the sea fogs. For lumber this tree is nearly as valuable as the sugar pine. From Eureka to San Diego, this is the material of which most of the houses are built. Because of its rich color and the high polish it takes, especially the curly and grained portions, its value for cabinet work is being more and more appreciated. On account of the presence of acid and the absence of pitch and rosin in its composition, it resists fire and is therefore a safe wood for building. When the Baldwin Hotel in San Francisco, a six-story building of brick and wood, burned down, two redwood water tanks on the top of the only brick wall that was left standing, were found to be hardly charred and quite water-tight.

It is the redwood which furnishes the largest boards for the lumber trade. Not long ago a man in the lumber region built his office of six boards taken from one of the trees. The boards were twelve by fourteen feet, and there was one for each wall, one for the floor, and one for the ceiling. Windows and doors were cut out where desired.

In the heart of the redwood and pine forests there are some thirty mill plants, and they own about half of the timber district. The methods of lumbering are exceedingly wasteful. Scarcely half of the standing timber of a tract is taken by the loggers and what is left is often burned or totally neglected. Replanting is unthought of and the young trees are treated as a nuisance.

Three fourths of the forests of California grow upon side hills, generally with an incline of from fifteen to thirty degrees. When the trees are gone, therefore, the rain soon washes away the soil, leaving the rocks bare. When the next rainy season comes, the water, not being able to sink into the earth, and so gradually find its way to the streams, rushes down the hillsides in torrents, flooding the smaller water courses. Then the rivers rise and overflow, causing great damage to property; but their waters quickly subside, and when the dry season comes they have not sufficient depth for the passage of ships of commerce. The total destruction of the forests would soon destroy the navigability of the principal water highways of the state, while another serious result would be the lessening of the water supply for irrigation.

The second variety of the Sequoia, the gigantea, or "big tree," as it is called, grows much farther inland than the redwood, being found on the western slopes of the Sierras. There are ten separate groves of these trees, from the little company of six in southern Placer County to the southernmost Sequoia, two hundred and sixty miles away on the Tule River. The whole put together would not make more than a few hundred thousand of extra-sized trees, and of the giants themselves not more than five hundred. These rise as high as three hundred and fifty feet, and are from twenty to thirty feet through. Near the Yosemite the stage road passes through the hollow center of one of those monsters. In a grove owned by the government some cavalry men, with their horses, lined up on a "big tree" log, and it easily held fourteen, each horse's nose touching the next one's tail.

How old these trees may be is yet unsettled, but Mr. John Muir, their intimate friend and companion, tells of one which was felled which showed by its rings that it was 2200 years old. Another which had blown down was fully 4000 years old. Later investigation makes it seem not unlikely that some have existed for even 5000 years. It seems a sin to destroy a living thing of that age.

The great basin of the Santa Cruz Mountains, which contains a large collection of the Sequoia sempervirens, belongs to the United States government. So, too, do the Mariposa grove of Sequoia gigantea, and the General Grant park, and Tuolumne grove, each of which contains a small number of fine specimens of the big trees. These properties will be protected, but all other groves, in which are the giant Sequoias, are in great danger. There has recently been a movement by the government toward purchasing the Calaveras grove, which has the finest collection of the big trees known, but nothing decided has been done. Meantime there are a number of mills engaged in devouring this noble forest.

Unless the people of California take up the matter with earnestness and energy, the state and the United States will stand disgraced before mankind for letting these wonders of the world, these largest and oldest of all living things, be destroyed for the lumber they will make. They should be purchased by the government and protected, then some movement should be started in all lumber districts by which waste in logging may be done away with, young trees protected and cleared, and forest land replanted with suitable trees. The law excluding cattle and sheep from the forests is already proving its wisdom by the new growth of young trees. Only among the giant Sequoias of the Tule and King's River district are there to be found baby trees of that species.

The lumber trade is one of the most interesting and necessary industries of the state. Work in the camp is healthful and well paid. Many a delicate boy or young man in the city would grow strong and healthy and live a much longer time if he would cast his lot with the hardy choppers and cutters of the great forest of the Pacific slope. A logging crew consists of thirty men, including two cooks. The discipline is as rigid as that of a military system; each man knows his own particular duties, and must attend to them promptly and faithfully. Trees are not chopped down, as used to be the custom; with the exception of a little chopping on either edge, a saw run by two men does the work. Oxen are seldom used, as in early days on the Atlantic coast, to haul out the logs, for they have given way to "donkeys,"--not the long-eared, loud-voiced little animals, but the powerful, compact donkey-engines.

Lumber schooners and steamers are the chief features of our coast traffic. Almost all the large cities of the Pacific coast owe their foundation and prosperity to this trade. San Francisco and Eureka in Humboldt County are the principal ports of the trade. Mendocino has a rock-bound coast, with no harbors, but she has fine forests. Here the lumber steamer secures its cargo by means of suspended wire chutes as trolleys. The outer end of the trolley wire is anchored in the ocean, the wire crosses the deck of the moored steamer, the slack being taken up to the ship's gaff, thus making a tight wire up and down which the trolley car with its load is sent.

Sometimes a great raft made of lumber is taken in tow by a steamer loaded with the same material and they start on a voyage down the coast, but this is a dangerous venture. If the sea becomes rough the raft may break loose from the steamer and go plunging over the waves, no one knows where. The brave captains of our coasting vessels fear nothing so much as a timber raft adrift which may crash into a vessel at any moment and against which there is no way of guarding.

Chapter XIII
To All that Sow the Time of Harvest Should be Given

In all but savage countries, wheat is the most important product of the soil, A large proportion of human beings living on the earth to-day are so poverty-stricken as to make the question of food a matter of anxiety for every day. The prayer for bread unites more voices than any other.

The padres who settled California understood this well. A number of bushels of wheat, snugly incased in leather sacks, formed a precious part of the cargo of the San Carlos, that stout Spanish vessel which in 1769 brought the first settlers to California. This seed-wheat was divided among the early missions and as soon as possible was planted-- not with success at first. For a time the padres made little progress in crop raising. They had to learn by their failures. In San Diego the first wheat planted was sown in the river bottom and the seed was carried entirely away by the rising of the stream in the winter; and the next year, which proved to be a dry one, it was planted so far from the water that it was almost all destroyed by drought. At San Gabriel the first crop was drowned out, but the second, planted on the plain where it could be irrigated, was a success. San Gabriel was chief among the missions for wheat raising, and was called the "mother of agriculture."

Grain planting and harvesting, in the days of the padres, differed widely from the methods which prevail to-day. Then the ground was plowed once or twice, but in what manner? A yoke of oxen, guided by an Indian, dragged a plow with an iron point made by an Indian blacksmith. If iron could not be obtained, the point was of oak. Seed, which had been first soaked in lye, was sown by hand, broadcast, and harrowed in with branches of trees. The grain was cut by the Indians with knives and sickles. It was afterward placed on the hardened floor of a circular corral made for the purpose, and into it was turned a band of horses which were urged to a run by the shouts and whips of the Indian vaqueros. After running one way they were frightened into turning and going the other. In this manner the grain was trampled out of the husks. It was freed from the chaff by being thrown high in the air by the shovelful, when the wind was blowing hard enough to carry away the light straw.

Next, the grain was washed and dried, then ground, generally between two stones bolted together. A pole for a handle was also fastened by the bolt, and the stone was turned, sometimes by mules, sometimes by Indians. La Perouse, the French scientist who visited the coast in 1786 and gave to the padres of San Carlos a handmill for grinding grain, said that it would enable four Indian women to do the work of a hundred by the old way. Before many years the padres at San Gabriel built a water mill of stone and adobe which ground grain in large quantities, but not with entire success, until Chapman, the first American in that region, gave them his assistance to perfect the machinery. This interesting building has been restored by Mr. H. E. Huntington and is an object of interest to those who visit San Gabriel.

In 1815 the missions raised enough wheat to supply the whole population, and there was even an attempt to ship grain to Mexico. This was a failure, but a little grain was sold to the Russians at Fort Ross. At the time of the change in the mission settlements, when the padres were sent away, all agriculture declined. During the Mexican War and when the crowd of gold seekers came, there was very little grain or flour to be had. Some of the gold hunters, who had been farmers in the East, failing to find a fortune in the river sands, and seeing the lack of food stuffs, went back to their old occupation. They put in crops of wheat and barley along the waters of the Sacramento and San Joaquin, and were amazed at the fertility of the soil and the success of their venture.

From this time the cultivation of wheat increased rapidly. In 1899 was harvested the largest crop recorded. After that there was a decline in wheat raising, because many farmers planted much of their grain lands to fruit for canning and drying. To California inventors is due the credit of substituting steam for hand labor in planting and harvesting grain.

Let us look at the busy scene on a grain field in the California of to-day. It is fall or early winter, and the time for planting has arrived. Into the field, which is several thousands of acres in extent, comes a great engine, one that does not need a track to run upon. Over the ground it rolls. With strength equal to fifty horses it draws behind it sixteen ten-inch plows, four six-foot harrows, and a press drill to match. It takes only a few men to manage it, and in a short time it has plowed, harrowed, and sown the broad acres; nothing is left to do until the harvest time arrives.

When the grain is ripe, there comes another great machine. This is the harvester, whose knives or cutters may be as much as twenty-six feet wide. This one machine cuts off the heads of wheat, thrashes them, cleans the grain, and sacks it, clearing seventy-five acres in a day, leaving on the fields the piles of sacked wheat ready for market. It is most interesting to watch one of these giants of steel and iron traveling over the uneven ground, crossing ditches, crawling along side hills, without any trouble or change of pace, gathering in the ripe grain, turning it out snugly tucked away in the brown gunny-sacks waiting for its long journey by ship or car. How the padres would wonder if they could see it working!

The grain of the California wheat is white and soft, and contains much gluten. No matter what hard red or yellow varieties are brought from other countries and planted here, in a year or two they change to the California type. It is not certainly known what causes this peculiarity. The grain most in favor through the state is called "club wheat" from the form of the head, which is blockshaped, instead of long and slender. The "club wheat" holds fast its grain so that it can be harvested without falling to the ground, which, in so dry a climate, is a great point in its favor.

Wheat is raised all over the state, both on high and on low land. Some of the largest grain ranches are along the tule lands around Stockton. These were marshes once, but have been drained, and now are choice grain fields. Wheat was first sent out of the state to England as ballast for returning ships, but the trade gradually increased until there are now over one hundred of the finest sailing vessels engaged in it. Unfortunately, few of these vessels are American, perhaps but one fourth. It is a pity that our countrymen should not benefit more by this trade. During the grain season at most of the Pacific ports the flag of nearly every nation on earth is represented. All styles of shipping, from the largest modern steamer to the smallest ocean sailing vessel, are then to be found in the harbors of the coast.

Grain is carried to the docks in barges, schooners, or on cars, and is seldom shipped except in sacks. Wheat, unless it needs to be cleaned or graded, is kept in the sack in which it leaves the home field. To watch the grain being loaded in the ship is a sight well worth seeing. If the wharf, or car, or warehouse where it lies is higher than the deck of the vessel on which it is to be shipped, the sacks are placed on an inclined chute down which they descend to the hold of the ship. If the deck of the vessel is the higher, sometimes an endless belt, run by electricity, is placed in a chute, the sacks are laid on the belt, and so carried to their resting place.

In loading wheat for export, a number of sacks in each row are bled; that is, a slit is made in the sack which allows a small quantity of grain to escape and fill the spaces round the corners and sides of the sack, thus making a compact cargo which is not liable to shift. At Port Costa is located a grader, where, when necessary wheat can be cleaned and graded; here also are many large warehouses.

For a long time about two thirds of the wheat crop of the state was sent to Ireland, but now our new lands in the Pacific take much of it. California has an immense trade in wheat that has been ground into flour. Over six million dollars' worth of flour is shipped each year, nearly three fourths of it going to China, Japan, and the islands of the Pacific.

It is believed by scientific agriculturists that better results will be obtained in wheat raising as smaller ranches become the rule, where the farmer can give more attention to the needs of the grain, adding what is necessary to the soil. Often the alternation of crops increases the yield--wheat doing much better if planted where beans or other legumes were raised the year before. Where the grain fields are not so large, irrigation can be depended upon instead of the rainfall, and crops then are sure and more even in quantity.

Barley is the grain next in importance to wheat in California. It can be raised where wheat can not, as it needs less moisture for its development; and if the rains fail, it can be cut for hay which always brings a good price. Barley hay, with the heads on, is in California the chief food of horses, and in many cases of cattle. A horse for ordinary work fed on barley hay gets all the grain necessary. If on account of heavier work, stronger food is required, rolled barley is given in addition. A large quantity of the better graded barley grain raised in the state is used by the brewers for malt.

Corn does not do so well through the state in general, but in some locations it is justly claimed that a man can ride on horseback down the rows of corn without being seen over the tops. This, too, the padres brought into the state. The tortilla, the common food of the Spanish settlers, was made of coarse-ground or pounded corn.

Alfalfa, the wonderful forage plant of dry regions of the West, is a member of the clover family. Throughout the southern and middle portion of California are large ranches devoted to its culture for hay. It is also raised extensively for green feed for horses and cattle. It produces from three to six crops a year according to location and care given it, and is treated for the market much the same as barley hay, except that it is generally made into smaller bales. Alfalfa is raised by irrigation, the best method being from flumes opening into indentations, not so deep as furrows, from which the water spreads, flooding the whole surface.

Many a California young man from high school gets his first taste of work away from home in the harvest fields. Generally this is a good experience for him. He receives some pretty hard knocks, and sees the rough side of life, but if he has self-control and good principles, he will be the better for the venture, returning more manly, earnest, and self-reliant.

Chapter XIV
The Golden Apples of the Hesperides

The orange, like many other of California's most valuable products, was brought into the country by the patient, far-seeing padres. Orange, lemon, and citron, those three gay cousins of royal blood, traveled together, and soon were to be found in many of the mission gardens. The most extensive of that early planting was an orchard at San Gabriel, set out by Padre Sanchez in 1804. In the height of its prosperity, this mission is recorded as having two thousand three hundred and thirty-three fruit trees, a large proportion of which were orange trees. San Fernando had sixteen hundred trees. San Diego had its orange orchard: how many trees is not recorded, but its olive grove numbered five hundred and seventeen flourishing trees. Santa Inez had nearly a thousand trees. As early as 1800 Santa Barbara and San Buenaventura also had valuable orchards.

Outside the missions the first orange trees in any number were planted in 1834, the famous Wolfskill grove in 1841. By 1862 there were about twenty-five thousand trees of this variety in the state, and two thirds of these belonged to Wolfskill, of Los

Angeles. A little later several large orchards were planted in the region around the Mission San Gabriel. In Riverside, often called the mother of orange culture in the state, the first seeds were planted in 1870, the first trees from these seeds in 1873, and from that period is dated the beginning of extensive planting. This was largely the work of colonists. About the time the orchards came into bearing, the Southern Pacific and the Santa Fe Overland were completed, so that an Eastern market was gained for the fruit, with the result that the new industry fairly bounded forward. So much was sometimes made from an acre of trees that it seemed as though people could not get land and plant fast enough. Occasionally an income was reported of three thousand dollars from an acre, and eight hundred to one thousand dollars per acre was not an uncommon crop.

Although at this time there were a few orange trees in the middle and northern parts of the state, for many years it was supposed that only the southern country could raise this fruit suitable for the market, but to-day people know better. Excellent oranges are grown as far north as Shasta, and Butte County, which leads in the northern orange culture, has a number of large and valuable orchards. From Tulare County and other parts of the valley of the San Joaquin, choice fruit is being shipped to the markets of the East. From San Diego all the way up the state one may find trees of the citrus family flourishing; still, whether north or south, in planting an orange orchard, the greatest care has to be taken in the choice of location. Jack Frost is the enemy to be avoided, and generally in any strip of country the lower lands are the ones he visits first. So the highlands are preferred, and even here the currents of air must be studied. A strong, uninterrupted, downward sweep of air from the snowcovered mountains will often, at night, drive away the needed warmth gathered during the day, so that land protected by some mountain spur which makes an eddy in the current is the best for this heat-loving fruit.

There are several popular varieties of the orange. The Valencia late is being planted by many in preference to others because, besides being a fine fruit, it keeps well, ripening when the days begin to be long and hot, and is therefore doubly welcome. The sweet orange from the Mediterranean country, and the St. Michael, with its paper rind, are also favorites, as are the delicious little Mandarin and Tangerine varieties, with their thin skin and high flavor; but the king of them all is the Washington navel, which has gained for the state its high position as an orange-raising territory. This is not a new variety, though many may believe it so. A book published in Rome over three hundred years ago gives an interesting description and pictures of this and other kinds of oranges and the way they should be raised. The title of this rare old volume is "Hesperides, or about the Golden Apples, their Culture and Use." Among its many fine illustrations is one of Hercules receiving the golden apples. Another shows the bringing of the fruit to Italy by a body of nymphs and goddesses in Neptune's car. Mr. Charles F. Lummis has translated portions of the book in the California magazine Out West.

On its travels the navel orange finally reached Bahia, Brazil, and there, sometime during the Civil War in the United States, a lady who, it is said, was the wife of the American consul, discovered the deliciousness of this fruit. So pleased was she that she determined to share her enjoyment with others; so upon her return to her own country, she described this orange to Mr. Saunders, head of the government's experimental farm at Washington. He became interested in the subject, sent to Bahia, and had twelve navel trees propagated by budding. These were shipped to Washington, where they arrived safely, and were placed in the orangery there. They all grew, and from them a large number of trees were budded.

Still they had not reached California. Bringing them to the Pacific coast was also the work of a woman. Mrs. Tibbetts, wife of a fruit grower of Riverside, was visiting in Washington and to her Mr. Saunders presented two navel orange trees, which she brought home with her. They were planted beside her doorstep in Riverside. The trees grew rapidly, and when they bore fruit it did not take the California orange growers long to discover that here they had a treasure of more value than the largest nugget of gold ever found in the state.

It was at a citrus fair in Riverside in 1879 that this golden king first appeared before the world. Then from all over southern California came orange men to get buds from these trees. Back home they went with the precious bits of life. Acres of seedling oranges were quickly shorn of their green crowns. Cut, cut, went knife and shears till only the stock was left, and then into a carefully made slit in the bark was placed the navel bud. It soon sprouted, and everywhere one could see the stranger growing sturdily on its adopted stem. Thousands of buds were sold from the two parent trees until there were hundreds of thousands of their beautiful children growing all over the state, giving golden harvests.

If we owe to two ladies the success of orange culture in California, it was a third who saved the industry when ruin threatened it. For a while all went merrily with the orange grower; then in some way, from Australia, there came into the country an insect pest called the cushiony scale, which settled on the orange trees and seemed likely to destroy them. "What can be done to save our trees?" was the cry from the people of the southland. What they did was to bring from Australia a different visitor, the dainty bug called the ladybird. She was eagerly welcomed. No one dreamed of bidding her, in the words of the old nursery rhyme, "fly away home." She was carried to the diseased orchards, where she settled on the scale, and as it was her favorite food, she soon had the trees clean again. In time other pests came to trouble vine and fruit growers, but it is interesting to know that scientists nearly always succeeded in finding some insect enemy of the troublesome visitor, which would help the horticulturist out of his difficulties.

In the business of orange-growing, success is due in a large measure to care in the picking, packing, and shipping of the fruit--care even in those little things that seem almost of no consequence. The more particular Californians are to ship only the best fruit in the best condition and properly packed, the higher prices will the fruit bring, the higher reputation the state gain.

The lemon industry comes closely second to the orange. This fruit does not need so much heat as does the orange, but neither can it stand so much cold. It needs more water, but it bears more fruit and can be marketed the year round. The lemons not sold as fresh fruit are made to yield such products as citric acid, oil of lemon, from which cooking essences are made, and candied lemon peel. In this latter branch of the trade, however, the citron is more generally used, though it is not of so delicate a flavor.

The pomelo, or grape fruit, is fast gaining in favor and increasing in value.

To the stranger who visits California the orange is the most interesting of trees. To pick an orange with her own hands, and to pin on her breast a bunch of the fragrant blossoms, is to an Eastern woman one of the most pleasant experiences of her visit to the Golden State.

In the history of the growth of southern California, and especially of its orange culture, the use of water on the soil plays a prominent part. It was the discovery that the most sandy and unpromising-looking land became a miracle of fertility when subjected to the irrigating stream, that caused the wonderful prosperity of the dry portions of the state.

Irrigation, which means the turning of water from a well, spring, or stream, upon land to promote the growth of plant life, has been used by mankind for thousands of years. In Colorado, Arizona, and New Mexico, there are remains of irrigation canals made by people who lived so long ago that we know nothing of their history.

The padres who settled California were adepts in this science. In founding a mission they always chose its site near some stream, the water of which could be turned upon the cultivated fields; and the dams, canals, and reservoirs which the padres constructed were so well built that many of them have lasted until the present time.

It will seem strange to many people to learn that the highest-priced, most fertile farm lands in the United States are not to be found in the rich valleys of the Eastern states or the prairies of the middle West, but in the dry region between the Rocky Mountains and the Pacific Ocean. Colorado, which belongs to the land of little rain, has in proportion to its size the richest mines of any state in the Union, yet the product of its farms, all irrigated, equals the output of its mineral wealth.

All the flourishing towns of southern California depend for their wonderful prosperity upon the fertility of the irrigated country surrounding them.

Trees and plants require water for their growth, but they do not all need it in like quantity, nor at the same time; therefore, the scientific farmer on arid lands, where there is an abundance of water for irrigation, has an immense advantage over his Eastern brother who depends for water upon the rainfall alone.

While the valuable raisin crop of the Californian is drying in the sun and the slightest shower would damage, or perhaps ruin it, just beyond lies the orange orchard, the trees of which are suffering for water. The fruit, the size of a large walnut, is still hard and green, and must have an abundance of the life-giving liquid if it is to develop into the rich yellow orange, filled with delicious juice, which adorns the New Year's market. How would our ranchman prosper if he depended upon rain? As it is, he furrows his orchard from its highest to its lowest level; then into the flume which runs parallel with the highest boundary of the grove he turns the water from pipe or reservoir, and opening the numerous little slide-doors or sluice-gates of the flume, soon has the satisfaction of seeing each furrow the bed of a running stream, the water of which sinks slowly, steadily, down to the roots of the thirsty trees. After the water has been flowing in this manner for some hours, it is shut off, for it has done enough work. In a day or two the ranchman runs the cultivator over the ground of the orchard, leaving the soil fine and crumbly and the trees in perfect condition for another six or eight weeks of growth.

The first attempts of the American immigrant at irrigation were very simple-- just the making of a furrow turning the water of a stream upon his land. Then, as he desired to cultivate more land and raise larger crops, his ditches had to be longer, often having branches. Soon neighbors came in and settled above and below him. They too used of the stream; there was no law to control selfishness, so there were disagreements and bitter quarrels over the water. Lawsuits followed and sometimes even fighting and murders. The remedy for this state of things was found to be in a company ditch, flume, or reservoir, with the use of water controlled by fixed laws.

There are some crops, notably grapes, which are grown without irrigation. The grapevine, instead of being treated as a climber, is each year trimmed back to the main stem, which thus becomes a strong woody stalk, often a foot or more in circumference, quite capable of withstanding the heat and dryness of the atmosphere and of drawing from the soil all the nourishment needed for the fruit.

Wheat, barley, and oats, both as grain and as hay, are largely raised without irrigation. Olives, and many deciduous trees, by careful cultivation may flourish without water other than the rainfall; yet notwithstanding this, for a home in southern California, land without a good water-right is of little value.

The wealth of the region is in a great measure in its expensive water system, which, by means of reservoirs, dams, ditches, flumes, and pipes, gathers the water from the mountain streams and conveys it to the thirsty land below.

Chapter XV
California's other Contributions to the World's Bill of Fare

By 1874 people in the Eastern states had begun to talk of California canned fruits. Apricots and the large white grape found ready sale, but California raisins, though on the market, were not in demand. That line from the old game "Malaga raisins are very fine raisins and figs from Smyrna are better," represented the idea of the public; and figs, raisins, and prunes eaten in the United States all came from abroad. But how is it to-day?

Thanksgiving and Christmas dinners of our Eastern friends owe much to California. She sends the seedless raisins, candied orange and lemon peel, the citron and beet sugar for the mince pies and plum puddings. Her cold-storage cars carry to the winter-bound states the delicious white celery of the peat lands, snow-white heads of cauliflower, crisp string beans, sweet young peas, green squash, cucumbers, and ripe tomatoes. For the salads are her olives and fresh lettuce dressed with the golden olive oil of the Golden State. Of ripe fruits, she sends pears, grapes, oranges, pomegranates. For desserts, she supplies great clusters of rich sugary raisins, creamy figs, stuffed prunes, and soft-shelled almonds and walnuts. All these and other delicacies California gives toward the holiday making in the East.

But it is not only to the homes of the wealthy that she carries good cheer; to people who have very little money to spend, and those who are far away from civilization, as soldiers, surveyors, woodmen, and road-builders, California's products go to help make palatable fare. To these her canned meats, fish, and vegetables, and canned and dried fruits, are very welcome.

The canneries and fruit-packing establishments of the state bring in many millions of dollars each year and give employment to a host of people, a large number of whom are women and young girls.

Most of the fruits California now raises came into the country with the padres. Captain Vancouver tells us that he found at the Santa Clara mission, at the time of his visit in 1792, a fine orchard consisting of apples, pears, peaches, plums, apricots; and at San Buenaventura all these with the addition of oranges, grapes, and pomegranates. Alfred Robinson describes the orchards and vineyards of San Gabriel mission as very extensive. Wine and brandy were made at most of the missions, San Fernando being especially noted for its brandy. Guadalupe Vallejo tells of bananas plantains, sugar cane, citrons, and date palms growing at the southern missions. Palm trees were planted "for their fruit, for the honor of St. Francis, and for use on Palm Sunday."

Not only did the padres enjoy fresh fruits from their gardens, but raisins were dried from the grapes, citron, orange, and lemon peel were candied, and much fruit was preserved. It is not recorded that they had pumpkin pie in those days, but a small, fine-grained pumpkin was raised extensively for preserves. It is still a favorite dainty among the native Californians, and no Spanish dinner is complete without this dulce, as it is called. Spanish-American housewives excel their American sisters in the art of preserving. Pumpkin, peach, pear, fig, are all treated in the same manner, being first soaked in lye, then thoroughly washed and scalded in abundance of fresh water, and then cooked in a very heavy sirup. The result of this treatment is that the outside of the fruit is crisp and brittle, while the inside is creamy and delicious.

The first of California's dried fruits to come before the public was the raisin. Raisins are merely the proper variety of grapes suitably dried. Some think that they are dipped in sugar, but this is not the fact. The only sugar is that contained in the juice of the grape, which should be about one fourth sugar. The only raisin grape for general use is the greenish variety called the Muscat. The rich purple or chocolate color of the raisin of the market is caused by the action of the sun while the raisin is being cured. If dried in the shade the fruit has a sickly greenish hue. The seedless Sultana is a small grape, fast coming into favor for a cooking raisin.

The proper planting of a raisin vineyard requires a large amount of care and labor. But the summer is one long holiday, as there is little to do to the vines from early May until August. Then comes picking time. From all the country round gather men and women, boys and girls, and the work begins.

To be a successful raisin grower and packer, one must take care in all little things. The workman who neglects to cut from the branch the imperfect or bad grapes, or who lays the fruit in the trays so that it will be in heaps or overlapped, is apt to be soon discharged. After about a week of exposure to the sun and air, the grapes are turned by placing an empty tray over a full one, and reversing the positions. Then after a few days longer in the sun, the fruit goes to the sweat-box, a hundred pounds to the box, and is placed in a room in the packing house, where it lies about ten days. The bunches go into this room unequally dried, with still a look and taste of grape about them, but after this sweating process they come out uniform in appearance, rich, sugary, tempting,--the raisins of commerce, with little suggestion of the fruit from which they came. Then they are boxed.

There are generally three grades: very choice clusters, ordinary and imperfect bunches, and loose raisins. Raisins of the third class are sent to the stemmer and a large proportion of them then go to the seeder. Seeding raisins for mother and grandmother at holiday times used to be the duty and pleasure of the older boys and girls of the household. But seeding is now done by machinery. A machine will seed on an average ten tons daily. Before entering the seeder the raisins are subjected to a thorough brushing, by which every particle of dust is removed. They are then run through rubber rollers which flatten the fruit and press the seeds to the surface; then through another pair of rollers, with wire teeth which catch and hold the seeds while the raisins pass on down a long chute to the packing room, where women and girls box them for market.

With all fruits the drying process is much the same, though peaches, apples, and pears are first peeled. California figs, when dried, sell well. This is a fruit which is growing in favor, whether fresh, preserved, or dried. Fruit canning is an interesting process. The fruit is not boiled in sirup and then placed in cans, as is frequently the custom in home preserving, but when peeled it is placed directly in the cans, in which it receives all its cooking and in which it is finally marketed.

The raising of beets and the converting of them into sugar form an industry which is growing rapidly, and is of the utmost importance to the people of the Pacific slope.

The canning of fresh vegetables is a new industry which is bringing into the state a steady stream of money, and in addition is proving a double blessing to thousands of people, both those who gain from it their living, and those who could not otherwise have vegetables for food. A sailor said recently that if he could not be a sailor he would do the next best thing--can vegetables for other sailors. When Galvez received the order from the king of Spain to found settlements in Upper California, one of the chief reasons for so doing was that fresh vegetables might be raised for the sailors engaged in the Philippine trade. To-day the Philippines use a large portion of California's canned goods.

In the southern counties olive orchards are being extensively planted. Near San Fernando is the largest in the world, covering thirteen hundred acres. Doctors have said that a liberal use of California olive oil will do much to promote the good health of mankind, and it is thought by many that the manufacture of olive oil will be one of the greatest industries the state has known.

Nut raising is keeping pace with fruit in importance. To an Eastern person it seems strange to see nut-bearing trees cultivated in orchards; though profitable, this method does away with the pleasures of nutting parties.

California's crystallized fruits are in constant demand, especially for the Christmas trade. This crystallizing is a process in which the juice is extracted and replaced with sugar sirup, which hardens and preserves the fruit from decay while still keeping the shape.

One sometimes reads the saying, "Fresno for raisins, Santa Clara for cherries and prunes, and the northern counties and mountain-ranches for apples." But in fact, California's fruit industries are well distributed over the state, and the really excellent work which is being done in all sections will still advance as the people learn more of the necessary details and methods.

In spite of mistakes and experiments the steady progress on the California ranches is being recognized. Of one of our leading fruit growers, Mr. Eliwood Cooper of Santa Barbara, the Marquis of Lorne writes in the Youth's Companion: "He has shown that California can produce better olive oil than France, Spain, or Italy, and English walnuts and European almonds in crops of which the old country hardly even dreams."

A history of California's products would be incomplete without a reference to him who is called the "Wonder Worker of Santa Rosa." "Magician! Conjurer!" are terms frequently applied to Mr. Luther Burbank, the man who is acknowledged by the scientists of the world to have done more with fruits and flowers than any other man. Mr. Burbank waves his wand, and the native poppy turns to deepest crimson, the white of the calla lily becomes a gorgeous yellow, rose and blackberry lose their thorns, the cactus its spines. The meat of the walnut and almond become richer in quality, while their shells diminish to the thinness of a knife blade.

Yet in these seeming miracles there is nothing of "black art" or sleight of hand. The experiments of this wonderful man, the surprising results he gains, are obtained, first by a close study of the laws of nature, then, where he desires change and improvement, by assisting her process, often through years of closest application and unceasing toil. He is a man of whom it is truthfully said, "He has led a life of hardships, has sacrificed self at every point, that he might glorify and make more beautiful the world around him." Any boy or girl who knows something of how plants grow and reproduce themselves will find great pleasure in following Mr. Burbank's simple methods.

It is only recently that his countrymen have begun to appreciate the work of this great naturalist. A short time ago a resident of Berkeley, a student and book-lover, one who knew Mr. Burbank but had given little attention to his productions, was in Paris. While there he had the good fortune to be present at a lecture delivered before a gathering of the most eminent scientists of Europe. In the course of his address the speaker had occasion to mention the name of Luther Burbank. Instantly every man in the audience arose and stood a moment in silence, giving to the simple mention of Mr. Burbank's name the respect usually paid to the presence of royalty. It is a name now known in all the languages of the civilized world, and numbers of the wisest of the world's citizens cross the ocean solely to visit the busy plant-grower of Santa Rosa.

Luther Burbank was born in Worcester, Massachusetts, in 1849, and while yet a lad his strongest desire was to produce new plants better than the old ones. His first experiment was with a vegetable. For the sake of getting seed, he planted some Early Rose potatoes in his mother's garden. In the whole patch only one seed-ball developed, and this he watched with constant care. Great was his disappointment, therefore, when one morning, just as it was ready to be picked, he found that it had disappeared. A careful search failed to recover the missing ball, but as he thought the matter over, while at work, it struck Luther that perhaps a dog had knocked it off in bounding through the garden. Looking more carefully for it, he found the ball twenty feet away from the vine on which it had hung. In it were twenty-three small, well-developed seeds. These he planted with great care, and from one of them came the first Burbank potatoes. The wealth of the country was materially increased by this discovery; the wealth of the boy only to the amount of one hundred and twenty-five dollars, which he used in attending a better school than he had before been able to enjoy.

In 1875 Mr. Burbank, to secure, as he said, "a climate which should be an ally and not an enemy to his work," moved to Santa Rosa, California. For ten years of poverty and severe toil he was engaged, for the sake of a livelihood, in the nursery business, making, in the meantime, such experiments as he had time for. During the next twenty years, however, Mr. Burbank was able to give nearly his whole time to his nature-studies. His energy is tireless, and his aim is to supply to humanity something for beauty, sustenance, or commerce better than it has possessed.

Perhaps among all his productions the greatest good to the world will arise from the spineless cactus. The scourge of the American desert is the cactus, commonly known as the prickly pear, the whole surface of which is covered with fine, needle-like spines, while its leaves are filled with a woody fiber most hurtful to animal life. When eaten by hunger-crazed cattle it causes death. After years of labor Mr. Burbank has succeeded in developing from this most unpromising of plants a perfected cactus which is truly a storehouse of food for man and beast. Spines and woody fiber have disappeared, leaving juicy, pear-shaped leaves, weighing often twenty-five or fifty pounds, which, when cooked in sirup, make a delicious preserve, and in their natural state furnish a nourishing, thirst-quenching food for domestic animals. The fruit of this immense plant is aromatic and delicate, and its seeds are at present worth far more than their weight in gold, since from them are to spring thousands of plants by means of which it is believed the uninhabitable portions of the desert may be made to support numberless herds of cattle.

Another of Mr. Burbank's achievements is the evergreen crimson rhubarb, which is not only far less acid than the old variety, but richer in flavor and a giant in size.

The pomato, a tomato grown on a potato plant, is most interesting. The plant is a free bearer, having a white, succulent, delicious fruit, admirable when cooked, used in a salad, or eaten fresh as our other fruit.

The experiments with prunes conducted at the Santa Rosa ranch have been of the greatest value to the state. For forty years the prune growers of the Pacific slope had been searching for a variety of this fruit which would be as rich in sugar and as abundant a bearer as the little California prune of commerce, and yet of a larger size, and earlier in its time of ripening. Mr. Burbank with his famous sugar prune filled all these requirements, and revolutionized the prune industry of the state. Besides this triumph he has succeeded in obtaining a variety of this fruit having a shell-less kernel, so that the fruit when dried much resembles those which are artificially stuffed.

The flowers which Mr. Burbank has evolved by his methods, and those which he has simply enlarged and glorified, are far too numerous to be named here.

In 1905 a grant of ten thousand dollars a year was bestowed upon Mr. Burbank by the Carnegie Institution of Washington, D.C., for the purpose of assisting him in his experiments. Seldom has money been better placed.

Chapter XVI
The Hidden Treasures of Mother Earth

Thousands of years ago, before the time of which we have any history, there were rivers in California,--rivers now dead,--whose sides were steeper and whose channels were wider than those of the rivers in the same part of the world to-day. Rapid streams they were, and busy, too; washing away from the rocks along their sides the gold held there, dropping the yellow grains down into the gravelly beds below. After a time there came down upon these rivers a volcanic outflow; great quantities of ashes, streams of lava and cement, burying them hundreds of feet deep, until over them mountain ridges extended for miles and miles.

Other changes in the earth's surface took place, and in the course of time our streams of to-day were formed. As they cut their way through the mountain ranges, some of them crossed the channels of old dead rivers, and finding the gold hidden there, carried some of it along, rolling it over and over, mixed with sand and gravel, down into the lower lands under the bright sunlight. Here it was found by Marshall and the gold hunters who followed him. These were the placer mines of which we read in Chapter VII.

Gradually the best placer mines were taken up and the newcomers to the gold fields traced the precious metal up the streams into the gravel of the hillsides. Then was begun hydraulic mining, where water did the work. In the canons great dams were constructed to catch the flow from the melting snows of the mountains, and miles of flumes were built to carry the water to the mining grounds. Immense pipes were laid and altogether millions of dollars were invested in hydraulic mining. The water coming down under heavy pressure from the mountain reservoirs passed through giant hose which would carry a hundred miner's inches, and, striking the mountain side with terrific force, washed away the earth from the rocks. Down fell the sand and gravel into sluices or boxes of running water where cleats and other arrangements caught and held the gold, which was heavy, while the lighter mixture was carried out into the canyon.

The material thus dumped on the mountain side was called debris, and to any one living in the mining region of the state that word means trouble --means fighting, lawsuits, ruin. For the debris did not stay up in the canyon, but was washed down into the rivers, overflowing farm lands, spoiling crops and orchards, and making the streams shallow, their waters muddy. So great was the destruction this process caused that, in 1893, the Congress of the United States enacted a law which provided for the creation of a Debris Commission to regulate the business of hydraulic mining in California. The result of the investigations of this commission was to put a stop to all hydraulic mining in territory drained by the San Joaquin and Sacramento rivers, or any other territory where the use of this form of mining should injure the river systems or lands adjacent. Thus, almost in a moment, the important industry was stopped.

It is estimated that over one hundred million dollars were invested in hydraulic mining. Much of this was entirely lost, as the expensive machinery rusted and the water system fell into ruins. It was very hard for the miners, as well as for the commerce of the state, but the act of the government was based upon the principle that one man's business must not damage another man's property. Clever engineers in the pay of the government are still trying to find some way by which the debris can be safely disposed of in order that this valuable system may resume operation.

Deprived of the use of water as their agent, gold hunters next tried mining by drifts; that is, by tunneling into the mountain's side until the bed of a buried river is reached. These tunnels are often five thousand to eight thousand feet long. The gold is brought out of the ground before it is washed clean of the gravel. Sometimes it is mixed with cement, when it has to be crushed in rollers before it can be cleared of other material. The counties where drift mining is most in operation are Placer, Nevada, and Sierra.

Quartz mining is the most expensive manner of getting out gold, and a great deal of valuable and complicated machinery has been invented for this branch of the business. The quartz mines of California are among the richest in the world, and some of the greatest fortunes of modern times have been made from them.

In a mine of this kind there is generally a shaft, or opening, extending straight down into the earth, from which, at different levels, passageways branch out where the veins of gold are richest. The openings must be timbered to prevent caving in, and there must be pumps to remove the water as well as hoisting works to take out the material. Then on the surface, as near as possible to the mouth of the mine, must be located the quartz mill. When possible, a tunnel is used in this mining, which makes the handling of ore less expensive, for then there need be no hoisting works or pumps, since the tunnel drains itself.

Gold in quartz rock is generally in ledges or veins, one to three feet in width. Digging it out is not very hard, save where there is not enough room to stand upright and use the pick, or when, in a shaft deep in the ground, the heat makes it difficult to work. A California boy at the mines wrote recently: "Mining is not so bad; that is, if I could get along without the occasional whack I bestow upon my left hand. Last week I started a little tunnel and pounded my hand so that it swelled up considerably. Drilling is not hard, and loading is a snap, but it's all interesting work and there is the excitement of seeing what you are going to find next."

When the ore reaches the surface it is sent to the mill, where it is first pulverized, then mixed with a chemical which goes about catching up the grains of gold--arresting and holding them fast. It is quite a long process before the gold is completely separated from all other material and ready for shipment. Often the quartz contains other minerals of value, the separation of which requires much work.

There is a very rich mine in Nevada called the Comstock, which some years ago had sunk its shafts so deep into the earth that it became almost impossible for the miners to work on account of the great heat, the bad air, and the quantity of water which had constantly to be pumped out. How these troubles were remedied is the story of one of California's greatest and best citizens. Adolph Sutro was a Prussian by birth, and his adopted state may well be proud to claim him. He had built a little quartz mill in Nevada, near the Comstock mine. Seeing the suffering of the workmen in all the mines on that mountain side, he thought of a plan for the construction of a large tunnel which was to begin at a low level at the nearest point of the Carson River and run deep into the mountain so that it could drain all the rich mining section, give good ventilation for the deep underground works, and afford a much cheaper and more convenient way of taking care of the ore. It was to be four miles long, with branches extending from it to different mines. Its height was to be ten feet; width, twelve, with a drainage trench in the center to carry away the waste water to the Carson River, and tracks on each side for the passage of mules and cars.

At first the mine owners were pleased with the project, and Mr. Sutro succeeded in forming a company to build the tunnel. Then he went to Washington, where the government became so interested in his plans that on July 25, 1866, there was passed an act of Congress granting Sutro such privileges in regard to public lands as would safeguard his work. About the time that the news of this action reached the West, the men who owned the mines and had made an arrangement for the use of the tunnel, decided that they did not want the work done; it is said, for the reason that they found Mr. Sutro too wise and far-seeing for them to be able to manage him. At all events, with all their wealth and power they tried to ruin him. They said that his plans were worthless, and any one was foolish to invest in the tunnel company. Then Mr. Sutro, by means of lectures upon the subject, appealed to the people. In California, Nevada, the Eastern states, and even Europe, he told what his plans would do for the miners and the good of the country. It was not long before he gained all the help he needed, and the great work was begun.

As the workmen progressed into the mountain side there were many difficulties to overcome. Day and night without ceasing the work went on. Laborers would faint from the combined heat and bad air, and be carried to the outer world to be revived. Carpenters followed the drillers, trackmen coming closely after. Loose rock, freshly blasted, was tumbled into waiting cars and hauled away over rails laid perhaps but half an hour before. Constantly in the front was Sutro himself, coat flung aside, sleeves rolled up. In the midst of the flying dirt, great heat, bad air, dripping slush, and slippery mud he worked side by side with the grimy, half-naked miners, thus showing himself capable not only of planning a great work, but of seeing personally that it was well done, no matter with what sacrifice to his own ease and comfort.

After the tunnel was completed, Mr. Sutro sold his interest in it for several millions of dollars. How that money was expended, any visitor to San Francisco well knows. With it were built the great Sutro baths, with their immense tanks of pure and constantly changing, tempered ocean water, their many dressing rooms, their grand staircases, adorned with rare growing plants, their tiers of seats rising in rows, one above another, with room for thousands of spectators, and their galleries of pictures and choice works of art. Over all is a roof of steel and tinted glass. Nowhere else in America is there so fine a bathing establishment.

Besides this there are the lovely gardens of Sutro Heights, developed by Mr. Sutro's money and genius from the barren sand-hills of the San Miguel rancho. In addition to these is the choice library of about two hundred thousand volumes, which is of great use to the people of San Francisco. Perhaps neither San Francisco nor California has yet quite appreciated the value of the work of Adolph Sutro.

Since 1848 the state of California has sent to the United States Mint over one billion dollars in gold. Of this, little Nevada County, which seems to be worth literally her weight in gold, has sent over two hundred and forty million. The Empire Mine is the leading producer of California, but there are others nearly as rich. Nevada City is in the center of this mining country. The streets are very hilly, and after a heavy rain people may be seen searching the city gutters and newly-formed rivulets for gold, and they are sometimes rewarded by finding fair-sized nuggets washed down from the hills above.

A visitor to one of the deep mines of California says:--

"We descended to the seven hundred foot level, where the day before a pile of ore had been blasted down. A little piece of the quartz, crushed in a mortar panned out four dollars in gold. I picked out one piece of rock, not larger than a peach, and the manager, after weighing and testing it, announced that it contained ten dollars in free gold. The kick of a boot would reveal ore which showed glittering specks of pure gold."

In the estimate of many people all very valuable mines are supposed to be of gold, but this is a mistake. While gold is king in California, copper mining is rapidly becoming of great importance. A continuous copper belt, the largest yet discovered in the world, exists under her soil, and while a comparatively small depth has been so far attained, the profit has been considerable. One of the largest quicksilver mines in the world is at New Almaden. The value of the output of the borax mines is over a million dollars a year. There were mined in California in 1907 over fifty different materials, most of them at a value of several thousand dollars a year, with some as high as a million and over.

The mineral product of California outranking gold in value is petroleum, which has added greatly to the wealth of the state. Natural gas and mineral waters are also valuable commercial products.

To many, the most interesting class among minerals is the gems, of which California yields a variety. The beautiful lilac stone, Kunzite, was discovered near Pala, San Diego County. This county has also some fine specimens of garnets, and beautiful tourmalines are being mined at a profit. San Bernardino County yields a superior grade of turquoise from which has been realized as much as eleven thousand dollars a year. Chrysoprase is being mined in Tulare County, also the beautiful new green gem something like clear jade, called Californite. Topaz, both blue and white, is being found, and besides these, many diamonds of good quality have been collected, principally from the gravels of the hydraulic mines. In 1907 there was discovered in the mountains of San Benito County a beautiful blue stone closely resembling sapphire, more brilliant but less durable. It was named, by professors of mineralogy in the state university, Benitite, from the place where it was discovered.

Perhaps the most valuable of all the products of California is its water supply, either visible as in springs and streams, or underground as in artesian water. Of its use in irrigation, we have already spoken. In the production of electricity it is coming to be of the greatest importance, making possible the most stupendous works of modern times. Such is the undertaking of the Edison Electric Company in bringing down to Los Angeles, over many miles of the roughest country, power from the Kern River, tapping the tumultuous stream far up in the Sierras. The taking of the necessary machinery to those heights was in itself a wonderful labor. The power thus created is a blessing to a wide region.

Chapter XVII
From La Escuela of Spanish California to the Schools of the Twentieth Century

In no line has California advanced so far beyond the days of the padres as in her schools. In the early settlements there were no educated people but the priests at the missions and the Spanish officers with their families at the presidios. Later, clever men of good families came into the territory, took up land, and made their homes on the great ranchos, but among these there were few who would take the time or trouble to teach the children; so life to the young people was a long holiday. The sad result was that they grew up so ignorant as to astonish the educated strangers who visited the coast.

At the missions the padres had schools where they taught the young Indians something of reading and writing, religious services and songs, and the trades necessary for life. This, with their duties in the church and the extensive building and planting of the mission settlements, took all the time of the hard-working priests. Occasionally, an educated woman would teach her own children and those of her relatives, but like most attempts at home education, it was so interrupted as to amount to little.

In 1794 a new governor came from Spain who was so shocked at this state of affairs that he at once ordered three schools opened. The first, December, 1794, was held in a granary at San Jose and was in charge of a retired sergeant of the Spanish army. The children had been so long free from all restraint that they did not like to go to school, and their parents did not always take the trouble to insist. There were some reasons for this, as the masters did not know much about what they were trying to teach, and the use of the ferule and scourge (the latter a whip of cords tipped with iron) was frequent and cruel. There were no books but primers, and these were hard to obtain. The writing, paper was furnished by the military authorities and had to be returned when the child was through with it, that it might be used in making cartridges. These schools were for boys only, girls not being expected to learn anything except cooking, sewing, and embroidery.

Slowly the state of things improved, and in 1829 in the yearly report to the Mexican government, it was stated that there were eleven primary schools in the province with three hundred and thirty-nine boys and girls. One of the best of these schools was that of Don Ignacio Coronel of Los Angeles.

In 1846 the first American school was opened at Santa Clara by Mrs. Oliver Mann Isbell. It provided for children from about twenty emigrant families and was held in a room of the Santa Clara mission on the great patio. The floor was of earth, the seats boxes; an opening in the tiled roof over the center of the room allowing the smoke to escape when, on rainy days, a fire was built on a rude platform of stones set in the middle of the floor. Wherever the Americans lived, they would have schools, although their first buildings were bare and inconvenient, with no grace or adornment either inside or out. In some out-of-the-way places, whole terms of school were spent most happily under spreading live oaks.

In the making of the first constitution, educational matters were not forgotten; one section providing that there should be a common school system supported by money from the sale of public lands. On account of the minerals the lands so allotted were supposed to contain, it was believed that they would sell for such vast amounts that the state would have money sufficient for the grandest public schools that ever existed. In fact these lands brought in altogether, after a number of years, less than a quarter of a million dollars. The act provided also that the schools be kept open three months in the year. An effort was made to extend this period to six months, but was defeated by Senator Gwin.

Considering the state of the country when the public schools were begun, and the short time in which they have been developed, the California free schools are a credit to the state and to the men and women who have helped to make them what they are. No community is so poor and remote but that it may have its school if the inhabitants choose to organize for the purpose. Hardly can the settler find a ranch from which his children may not attend a district school over which floats the stars and stripes.

Money for educational purposes is now raised by state and county taxes on property, this sum, in cities, being largely increased by the addition of the city taxes. High schools have only recently been given state aid, and that moderately;

the larger ones still depending, in a great measure, upon the special tax of the city, district, or county, according to the class to which the school belongs. The state supports one Polytechnic school, that at San Luis Obispo, where there are three courses, agriculture, mechanics, and domestic science.

About 1878, in the endeavor to teach the children of the worst parts of San Francisco a right way of living, the free kindergartens were begun. Perhaps their success cannot be better shown than in the fact that in the first year of the work along "Barbary coast," one of the most turbulent districts of the city, the Italian fruit and vegetable dealers who lived there, brought the teachers a purse of seventy-five dollars, because the children had been taught not to steal their fruits and vegetables or to break their windows. The first free kindergarten was started on Silver Street in "Tar Flats" and had for its teacher a pretty young girl, with beautiful eyes and a mass of bronze-colored hair, whom the ragged little urchins soon learned to adore. That little school was the beginning of one of the best kindergarten systems in the country, and the pretty young teacher is now Kate Douglas Wiggin, one of America's best loved writers, the author of those delightful books, "The Birds' Christmas Carol," "Timothy's Quest" and others equally interesting. There have been many gifts to these kindergartens. In memory of their only son, Mr, and Mrs. Leland Stanford gave one hundred thousand dollars, while Mrs. Phoebe Hearst supported entirely three of the schools. Kindergartens may now form part of the primary department in the school system of any community so desiring, and are to be found in most of the cities.

Nothing in the educational work of California is of more importance than the five normal schools, which graduate each year hundreds of teachers thoroughly prepared in all branches for the important work of training the children of the state.

As the crown of the free school system, stands the state university at Berkeley. Many an interesting story might be told of the noble men, who as early as 1849 began their long struggle to gain for the youth of California the chance for higher education. The Reverend Samuel Willey, the American consul Mr. Larkin, and Mr. Sherman Day were leaders in this enterprise. There was much against them; men's thoughts were almost entirely given to the necessities of everyday life, and few seemed able to see that a grand and beautiful future was coming to the new territory. The university secured its charter in 1868, but it was not until the adoption of the new constitution in 1879 that it was placed on a firm basis which could not be changed by each new legislature.

The coming of Mr. Benjamin Ide Wheeler to the presidency was one of the best strokes of fortune the institution has ever known. Under his management it has taken a great stride forward. In the work it does, and the high standard it demands, it takes its place side by side with the best universities of the older Eastern states. The work of its college of agriculture is becoming of great service to the farmer and fruit grower. The result of its experiments in determining the best wheat for the soil is of very great importance to the grain industry of the state.

Connected with the university are: the Lick Observatory on Mount Hamilton; the Mark Hopkins Institute of Art, the Hastings College of Law, and Colleges of Medicine, Dentistry, and Pharmacy, in San Francisco; and an admirable University Extension Course which offers its advantages to the people of any locality throughout the state who may desire its help.

One of the most practical and important associations in the state is the Farmer's Institute, which, under direction and control of the university, holds a three days' meeting once a month in each locality throughout the state. Also, once a year, an institute of a week's duration is held at Berkeley, where eminent scientists give their services, and the results are most helpful.

The university has received many gifts from distinguished citizens. Mrs. Phoebe Hearst has devoted much of her time and a large amount of her money to its improvement, and plans are under way to make it the most finished and beautiful educational institution ever owned by any state or country.

Barely one hour's ride from San Francisco south, lies the Leland Stanford Junior University, which at the time of its foundation, in 1885, was the greatest gift ever bestowed upon humanity by any one person. In this noble movement Mr. and Mrs. Stanford were as one. Their only son died in 1884, and the university is a memorial of him, a grand example of the way in which those who are dead may yet live, through the good done in their names. Although entirely a private benefaction, its doors are open to students absolutely free of all tuition charges.

This university started with a large endowment, but after the death of Mr. Stanford, a lawsuit with the United States, and a shrinkage in the value of the properties it owned, ran the finances so low that for a short time it was found necessary to charge a small entrance fee. Even then, the college was kept open only through the economy and self-sacrifice of Mrs. Stanford and the members of the faculty, who stood by the institution with noble unselfishness. By the year 1906 the financial condition had become satisfactory and the attendance had materially increased. Two handsome new buildings, one for the library and the other for the gymnasium, were about completed when, on April 18, an earthquake, the most destructive ever experienced on the Pacific coast, shook all the region around San Francisco Bay. Stanford suffered severely: the two new buildings were ruined; so, too, was the museum and a portion of the chemistry building. Both the noble arch and the mosaics in the front of the memorial chapel were destroyed. Beyond this, comparatively little damage was done to the college buildings. The graduating exercises were postponed until the fall term; otherwise the disaster did not interfere seriously with the routine of study, neither did it affect the attendance in 1906-7, which was unusually large. In the fall of 1907 President Jordan stated that he was empowered to announce that Thomas Weldon Stanford, brother of Senator Leland Stanford, had decided to give the university his own large fortune of several millions.

It is generally recognized that the university owes a great part of its present success to the splendid talents and faithfulness of President Jordan, who has given the hardest labor of the best years of his busy life to helping it onward and upward. Its educational work is thorough, and its requirements are being steadily raised. It stands for the highest education that is possible. Addition is constantly being made to its group of noble buildings. Beautiful Stanford is the sparkling jewel in California's diadem.

Not far from the University of California in the suburbs of Oakland is situated Mills College, which for many years was the only advanced school for girls of which the state could boast. This institution had its beginning as a seminary in Benicia, but was moved to its present situation in 1871. In 1885 it became a college with a state charter. In plan of studies and high Christian aim, it resembles Mount Holyoke, from which many of its leading instructors have been graduated.

There is no place here to speak of all the leading private schools of the state. Throop Polytechnic in Pasadena, the Thatcher School in the valley of the Ojai, and Belmont Military Academy are among the best. A word, however, must be said in tribute to Santa Clara College, without which the California youth of from twenty to forty years ago would have been lacking in that higher education which stands for so much in the making of a state. Incorporated in 1851, it was opened with funds amounting to but one hundred and fifty dollars, yet it grew steadily. With a clever Jesuit faculty, this college has done admirable work of so thorough a character as to win the praise of all those who have come in contact with its results. From it have been graduated such men as Stephen M. White, Reginaldo del Valle, and many other of our leading professional and business men.

Chapter XVIII
Statistics

The state of California lies between the parallels 32i and 42i north latitude, extending over a space represented on the eastern coast by the country between Edisto Inlet, South Carolina, and the northern point of Cape Cod, Massachusetts. Its northern third lies between 120i and 124i 26' west longitude. From Cape Mendocino, its most westerly point, the coast trends southeastward to San Diego Bay. The total coast line on the Pacific is 1200 miles.

The state's greatest width is 235 miles, which is between Point Conception and the northern end of the Amaragosa Range on the Nevada line. It is narrowest between Golden Gate and the southern end of Lake Tahoe. Its area is 158,297 sq. miles, second only to Texas of all the states.

The population of California, according to the United States census of 1920, is 3,426,861, which has since been greatly increased. The following table shows the counties of the State:--

Counties of California

Name	Area Sq. Mi.	Population 1920	Valuation 1910 of Property	Origin and Meaning of Name County Seat

Alameda   Sp., Shaded promenade
764 344,127 246,131 128,681,766 Oakland
Alpine
710   243   309   422,063 Markleeville
Amador   Sp., Sweetheart
632 7,793 9,086 4,918,908 Jackson
Butte   Fr., Rounded, detached hill
1,660 30,030 27,301 16,057,766 Oroville
Calaveras   Sp., Skul's (from Indian battle ground)
1,080 6,183 9,171 6,177,285 San Andreas
Colusa   Ind.
1,088 9,290 7,732 12,188,096 Colusa
Contra Costa   Sp., Opposite coast
728 53,889 31,674 21,753,956 Martinez
Del Norte   Sp., Of the North
992 2,759 2,417 2,882,445 Crescent City
Eldorado   Sp., The gilded (name given to fabled land of gold)
1,796 6,426 7,492 4,668,840 Placerville
Fresno   Sp., Ash tree
6,152 128,779 75,657 34,302,205 Fresno
Glenn
1,270 11,853 7,172 10,645,524 Willow
Humboldt   (named for Baron von Humboldt)
3,496 37,413 33,857 24,911,492 Eureka
Imperial
4,200 43,383 13,591   El Centro
Inyo
10,294 7,031 6,974 2,316,319 Independence
Kern
8,050 54,843 37,715 24,050,871 Bakersfield
Kings

1,176 22,032 16,230   7,883,009 Hanford
Lake
1,328 5,402 5,526   3,258,020 Lakeport
Lassen
4,520 8,507 4,802   4,590,748 Susanville
Los Angeles   Sp., The angels
4,200 936,438 504,132 169,268,166 Los Angeles
Madera   Sp., Timber
2,062 12,203 8,368   6,732,495 Madera
Marin   Ind.
549 27,342 25,114 14,489,582 San Rafael
Mariposa   Sp., Butterfly
1,510 2,775 3,956   2,270,246 Mariposa
Mendocino   Sp., (from Mendoza, viceroy of Mexico)
3,626 24,116 23,929 13,131,995 Ukiah
Merced   Sp., Mercy
1,932 24,579 15,148 14,877,086 Merced
Modoc   Ind.
3,741 5,425 6,191   4,076,680 Alturas
Mono   Sp., Monkey, or pretty
3,020   960 2,042   1,151,109 Bridgeport
Monterey   Sp., King's forest
3,340 27,980 24,146 18,962,554 Salinas
Napa   Ind.
780 20,678 19,800 13,840,291 Napa
Nevada   Sp., Heavy fall of snow
972 10,850 14,955   7,203,349 Nevada City
Orange   (named for its chief product)
750 61,375 34,436   13,812 Santa Ana
Placer   Sp., Loose (from placer mines)
1,365 18,584 18,237   9,677,724 Auburn
Plumas   Sp., Feathers
2,694 5,681 5,259   2,792,091 Quincy

Riverside
7,323 50,297 34,696 16,373,296 Riverside
Sacramento   Sp., The Sacrament
1,000 90,978 67,806 41,333,337 Sacramento
San Benito   Sp., St. Benedict
1,388 8,995 8,041 6,499,068 Hollister
San Bernardino Sp., St. Bernard
19,947 73,401 56,706 21,392,228 San Bernardino
San Diego   Sp., St. James
4,278 112,248 61,665 20,807,594 San Diego
San Francisco Sp., St. Francis (of Assisi)
47 506,676 416,912 564,070,301 San Francisco
San Joaquin   Sp., name of a saint
1,396 79,905 50,732 34,740,353 Stockton
San Luis Obispo Sp., St. Louis the Bishop
3,310 21,893 19,383 13,680,235 San Luis Obispo
San Mateo   Sp., St. Matthew
434 36,781 26,585 18,999,564 Redwood City
Santa Barbara   Sp., St. Barbara
2,632 41,097 27,738 18,849,976 Santa Barbara
Santa Clara   Sp., name of a saint
1,286 100,588 83,539 61,390,817 San Jose
Santa Cruz   Sp., Holy Cross
424 26,269 26,240 12,560,071 Santa Cruz
Shasta   Fr., Chaste, pure
3,876 13,311 18,920 10,902,036 Redding
Sierra   Sp., Sawtoothed Ridge
960 1,783 4,098 1,844,560 Downieville
Siskiyou
5,991 13,545 18,801 10,560,650 Treks
Solano   Sp., name of a mission
900 40,602 27,559 20,195,481 Fairfield
Sonoma   Ind., Valley of the Moon

1,620 51,990 48,394 30,380,419 Santa Rosa
Stanislaus
1,456 43,557 22,522 12,834,108 Modesto
Sutter   (named for J. A. Sutter)
622 10,115 6,328 6,621,047 Yuba City
Tehama
3,008 12,882 11,401 11,674,562 Red Bluff
Trinity
3,282 2,552 3,301 1,651,362 Weaverville
Tulare   Sp., Reed-covered
4,952 59,032 35,440 17,447,042 Visalia
Tuolumne   Ind., Stone wigwams
2,208 7,768 9,979 7,089,725 Sonora
Ventura   Sp.
1,722 28,724 18,347 11,171,219 Ventura
Yolo   Ind., Rushes
996 17,105 13,926 17,640,436 Woodland
Yuba   Sp., Uba, wild grapes
636 10,375 10,042 5,898,350 Marysville

List of Governors

Gaspar de Portola, April, 1769
Pedro Fages, July, 1770
Fernando Rivera y Moncada, May 25, 1774
Felipe de Neve, Feb. 3, 1777
Pedro Fages, Sept. 1O, 1782
Jose Romeu, April 16, 1791
Jose Arrillaga, April 9, 1792

Diego de Borica, May 14, 1794
Jose Arrillaga, Jan. 16, 1800
Jose Arguello, July 24, 1814
Pablo de Sola, March 31, 1815

California became province of the Mexican Empire, April 11, 1822

Luis Arguello, Nov. 10, 1822, First native Governor.

March 26, 1825, California became province of Mexican Republic.

Jose Maria Echeandia, Nov. 8, 1825
Manuel Victoria, Jan. 31, 1831
Jose Maria Echeandia, Dec. 6, 1831
Jose Figueroa, Jan. 15, 1833
Jose Castro, Sept. 29, 1835
Nicolas Gutierrez, Jan. 2, 1836
Mariano Chico, May 3, 1836
Nicolas Gutierrez, Sept. 6, 1836
Jose Castro, Nov. 5, 1836
Juan B. Alvarado, Dec. 7, 1836
Manuel Micheltorena, Dec. 31, 1842
Pio Pico, Feb. 22, 1845, to Aug. 10, 1846, end of Mexican rule.

The following were Governors under Military Rule, U.S.A.

John D. Sloat, July 7, 1846
Robert F. Stockton, July 29, 1846
John C. Fremont, Military Governor, Jan. 19, 1847, for 50 days
Stephen W. Kearny, Military Governor, March to May 31, 1847
R. B. Mason, Military Governor, May 31, 1847
Persifer F. Smith, Military Governor, Feb. 28, 1849
Bennet Riley, April 12, 1849

Peter H. Burnett, Dec. 20, 1849, First State Governor, Democratic, received 6716 votes, total vote, 12,064.
John McDougall, Lieutenant Governor, became Governor Jan. 9, 1851, Democrat
John Bigler, Jan. 8, 1852, Democrat
John Bigler, Jan. 7, 1854, Democrat
John Neely Johnson, Jan. 9, 1856, American Party
John B. Weller, Jan. 8, 1858, Democrat
Milton S. Latham, Jan. 9, 1860, Democrat
John G. Downey (Lieutenant Governor), inaugurated Jan. 14, 1860, Democrat
Leland Stanford, Jan. 10, 1862, Republican
Frederick F. Low, Dec. 10, 1863, Union Party
Henry H. Haight, Dec. 5, 1867, Democrat
Newton Booth, Dec. 8, 1871, Republican
Romualdo Pacheco (Lieutenant Governor), inaugurated Feb. 27, 1875, Republican (native state Governor)
William Irwin, Dec. 8, 1875, Democrat
Geo. C. Perkins, Jan. 8, 1880, Republican
Geo. Stoneman, Jan. 10, 1883, Democrat
Washington Bartlett, Jan. 8, 1887, Democrat
Robert W. Waterman (Lieutenant Governor), inaugurated Sept. 13, 1887, Republican
H. H. Markham, Jan. 8, 1891, Republican
James H. Budd, Jan. II, 1895, Democrat
Henry T. Gage, Jan. 4, 1899, Republican
Geo. C. Pardee, Jan. 7, 1903, Republican
James N. Gillett, Jan. 9, 1907, Republican
Hiram W. Johnson, January, 1911, Republican; reelected on Progressive ticket, 1914

William D. Stephens (Lieutenant Governor), inaugurated March 15, 1917, Progressive

Electoral Vote

1852, Democratic, 4 votes
1856, Democratic, 4 votes
1860, Republican, 4 votes
1864, Republican, 5 votes
1868, Republican, 5 votes
1872, Republican, 6 votes
1876, Republican, 6 votes
1880 Republican, 1 vote
    Democratic, 5 votes
1884, Republican, 8 votes
1888, Republican, 8 votes
1892, Republican, 1 vote
    Democratic, 8 votes
1896, Republican, 8 votes
    Democratic, People's and Silver parties, 1 vote
1900, Republican, 9 votes
1904, Republican, 9 votes
1908, Republican, to votes
1912, Democratic, 2 votes
    Progressive, 11 votes
1916, Democratic, 13 votes
1920, Republican, 13 votes

Bibliography

Bancroft--"History of California," vols. I, II, Ill, IV, V, VI, VII.
Bancroft--"California Pastoral."
Bancroft--"History of North Mexican States."
Hittell--"History of California," vols. I, II, III, IV.
Royce--"History of California."
Blackmar--"Spanish Institutions of the Southwest."
Montalvo--"Sergas of Esplandian." Translator, E. E. Hale, Atlantic
Monthly, Vol. XIII, p. 265.
Vancouver--"Voyage of Discovery to the Pacific Ocean," vol. III.
Geronimo Boscano--"Chinigchinich," "History of Mission Indians."
  Translator,
Alfred Robinson--"Life in California."
Francisco Palou--"Life of Fray Junipero Serra."
Junipero Serra--"Diary." Translated in magazine Out West, March-July,
  1902.
Hakluyt--"Drake's Voyages."
Vanegas--"History of California."
Davis--"Sixty Years in California."
Colton--"Three Years in California."
Fremont--"Memoirs."
Sherman--"Memoirs." Century Magazine, vols. 41-42.
Stoddard--"In the Footsteps of the Padres."
Lummis--"The Right Hand of the Continent." Series, Out West Magazine,
  1903.
Lummis--" Spanish Pioneers."
Jackson--"A Century of Dishonor."
Jackson--"Ramona."
California Book of Louisiana Purchase Exposition.

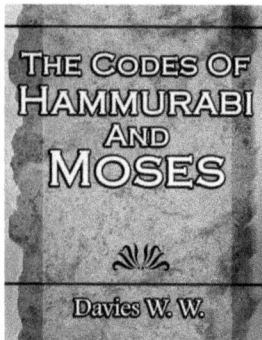

The Codes Of Hammurabi And Moses
W. W. Davies

QTY

The discovery of the Hammurabi Code is one of the greatest achievements of archaeology, and is of paramount interest, not only to the student of the Bible, but also to all those interested in ancient history...

Religion   **ISBN:** *1-59462-338-4*   **Pages:132**
                                                    MSRP $12.95

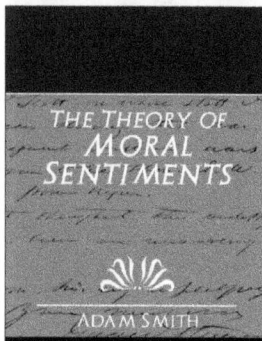

The Theory of Moral Sentiments
Adam Smith

QTY

This work from 1749. contains original theories of conscience amd moral judgment and it is the foundation for systemof morals.

Philosophy **ISBN:** *1-59462-777-0*   **Pages:536**
                                                    MSRP $19.95

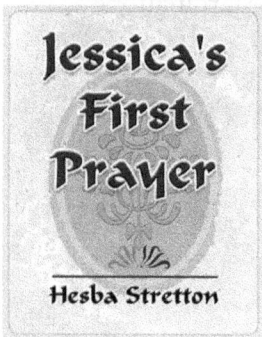

Jessica's First Prayer
Hesba Stretton

QTY

In a screened and secluded corner of one of the many railway-bridges which span the streets of London there could be seen a few years ago, from five o'clock every morning until half past eight, a tidily set-out coffee-stall, consisting of a trestle and board, upon which stood two large tin cans, with a small fire of charcoal burning under each so as to keep the coffee boiling during the early hours of the morning when the work-people were thronging into the city on their way to their daily toil...

                                                    Pages:84
Childrens   **ISBN:** *1-59462-373-2*   *MSRP $9.95*

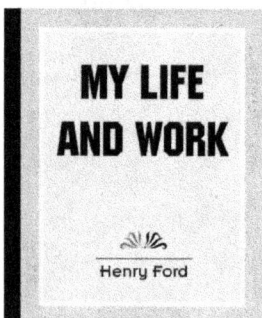

My Life and Work
Henry Ford

QTY

Henry Ford revolutionized the world with his implementation of mass production for the Model T automobile. Gain valuable business insight into his life and work with his own auto-biography... "We have only started on our development of our country we have not as yet, with all our talk of wonderful progress, done more than scratch the surface. The progress has been wonderful enough but..."

                                                    Pages:300
Biographies/ **ISBN:** *1-59462-198-5*   *MSRP $21.95*

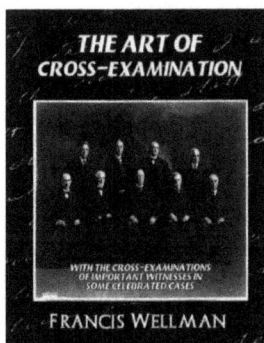

The Art of Cross-Examination
Francis Wellman

QTY

I presume it is the experience of every author, after his first book is published upon an important subject, to be almost overwhelmed with a wealth of ideas and illustrations which could readily have been included in his book, and which to his own mind, at least, seem to make a second edition inevitable. Such certainly was the case with me; and when the first edition had reached its sixth impression in five months, I rejoiced to learn that it seemed to my publishers that the book had met with a sufficiently favorable reception to justify a second and considerably enlarged edition. ..

Reference   **ISBN: *1-59462-647-2***

Pages:412

MSRP $19.95

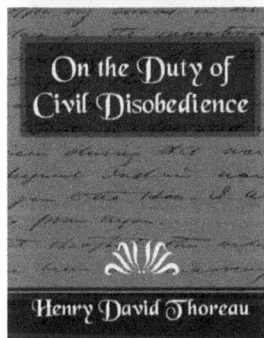

On the Duty of Civil Disobedience
Henry David Thoreau

QTY

Thoreau wrote his famous essay, On the Duty of Civil Disobedience, as a protest against an unjust but popular war and the immoral but popular institution of slave-owning. He did more than write—he declined to pay his taxes, and was hauled off to gaol in consequence. Who can say how much this refusal of his hastened the end of the war and of slavery ?

Law   **ISBN: *1-59462-747-9***

Pages:48

MSRP $7.45

Dream Psychology Psychoanalysis for Beginners
Sigmund Freud

QTY

Sigmund Freud, born Sigismund Schlomo Freud (May 6, 1856 - September 23, 1939), was a Jewish-Austrian neurologist and psychiatrist who co-founded the psychoanalytic school of psychology. Freud is best known for his theories of the unconscious mind, especially involving the mechanism of repression; his redefinition of sexual desire as mobile and directed towards a wide variety of objects; and his therapeutic techniques, especially his understanding of transference in the therapeutic relationship and the presumed value of dreams as sources of insight into unconscious desires.

Psychology   **ISBN: *1-59462-905-6***

Pages:196

MSRP $15.45

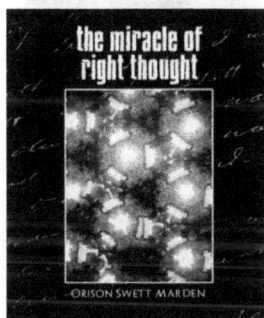

The Miracle of Right Thought
Orison Swett Marden

QTY

Believe with all of your heart that you will do what you were made to do. When the mind has once formed the habit of holding cheerful, happy, prosperous pictures, it will not be easy to form the opposite habit. It does not matter how improbable or how far away this realization may see, or how dark the prospects may be, if we visualize them as best we can, as vividly as possible, hold tenaciously to them and vigorously struggle to attain them, they will gradually become actualized, realized in the life. But a desire, a longing without endeavor, a yearning abandoned or held indifferently will vanish without realization.

Self Help   **ISBN: *1-59462-644-8***

Pages:360

MSRP $25.45

QTY

The Rosicrucian Cosmo-Conception Mystic Christianity by *Max Heindel*   ISBN: *1-59462-188-8*   **$38.95**
The Rosicrucian Cosmo-conception is not dogmatic, neither does it appeal to any other authority than the reason of the student. It is: not controversial, but is: sent forth in the, hope that it may help to clear...   *New Age/Religion Pages 646*

Abandonment To Divine Providence by *Jean-Pierre de Caussade*   ISBN: *1-59462-228-0*   **$25.95**
"The Rev. Jean Pierre de Caussade was one of the most remarkable spiritual writers of the Society of Jesus in France in the 18th Century. His death took place at Toulouse in 1751. His works have gone through many editions and have been republished...   *Inspirational/Religion Pages 400*

Mental Chemistry by *Charles Haanel*   ISBN: *1-59462-192-6*   **$23.95**
Mental Chemistry allows the change of material conditions by combining and appropriately utilizing the power of the mind. Much like applied chemistry creates something new and unique out of careful combinations of chemicals the mastery of mental chemistry...   *New Age Pages 354*

The Letters of Robert Browning and Elizabeth Barret Barrett 1845-1846 vol II   ISBN: *1-59462-193-4*   **$35.95**
by *Robert Browning* and *Elizabeth Barrett*
                                                                                                         Biographies Pages 596

Gleanings In Genesis (volume I) by *Arthur W. Pink*   ISBN: *1-59462-130-6*   **$27.45**
Appropriately has Genesis been termed "the seed plot of the Bible" for in it we have, in germ form, almost all of the great doctrines which are afterwards fully developed in the books of Scripture which follow...   *Religion/Inspirational Pages 420*

The Master Key by *L. W. de Laurence*   ISBN: *1-59462-001-6*   **$30.95**
In no branch of human knowledge has there been a more lively increase of the spirit of research during the past few years than in the study of Psychology, Concentration and Mental Discipline. The requests for authentic lessons in Thought Control, Mental Discipline and...   *New Age/Business Pages 422*

The Lesser Key Of Solomon Goetia by *L. W. de Laurence*   ISBN: *1-59462-092-X*   **$9.95**
This translation of the first book of the "Lernegton" which is now for the first time made accessible to students of Talismanic Magic was done, after careful collation and edition, from numerous Ancient Manuscripts in Hebrew, Latin, and French...   *New Age/Occult Pages 92*

Rubaiyat Of Omar Khayyam by *Edward Fitzgerald*   ISBN:*1-59462-332-5*   **$13.95**
Edward Fitzgerald, whom the world has already learned, in spite of his own efforts to remain within the shadow of anonymity, to look upon as one of the rarest poets of the century, was born at Bredfield, in Suffolk, on the 31st of March, 1809. He was the third son of John Purcell...   *Music Pages 172*

Ancient Law by *Henry Maine*   ISBN: *1-59462-128-4*   **$29.95**
The chief object of the following pages is to indicate some of the earliest ideas of mankind, as they are reflected in Ancient Law, and to point out the relation of those ideas to modern thought.   *Religion/History Pages 452*

Far-Away Stories by *William J. Locke*   ISBN: *1-59462-129-2*   **$19.45**
"Good wine needs no bush, but a collection of mixed vintages does. And this book is just such a collection. Some of the stories I do not want to remain buried for ever in the museum files of dead magazine-numbers an author's not unpardonable vanity..."   *Fiction Pages 272*

Life of David Crockett by *David Crockett*   ISBN: *1-59462-250-7*   **$27.45**
"Colonel David Crockett was one of the most remarkable men of the times in which he lived. Born in humble life, but gifted with a strong will, an indomitable courage, and unremitting perseverance...   *Biographies/New Age Pages 424*

Lip-Reading by *Edward Nitchie*   ISBN: *1-59462-206-X*   **$25.95**
Edward B. Nitchie, founder of the New York School for the Hard of Hearing, now the Nitchie School of Lip-Reading, Inc, wrote "LIP-READING Principles and Practice". The development and perfecting of this meritorious work on lip-reading was an undertaking...   *How-to Pages 400*

A Handbook of Suggestive Therapeutics, Applied Hypnotism, Psychic Science   ISBN: *1-59462-214-0*   **$24.95**
by *Henry Munro*
                                                                                           Health/New Age/Health/Self-help Pages 376

A Doll's House: and Two Other Plays by *Henrik Ibsen*   ISBN: *1-59462-112-8*   **$19.95**
Henrik Ibsen created this classic when in revolutionary 1848 Rome. Introducing some striking concepts in playwriting for the realist genre, this play has been studied the world over.   *Fiction/Classics/Plays 308*

The Light of Asia by *sir Edwin Arnold*   ISBN: *1-59462-204-3*   **$13.95**
In this poetic masterpiece, Edwin Arnold describes the life and teachings of Buddha. The man who was to become known as Buddha to the world was born as Prince Gautama of India but he rejected the worldly riches and abandoned the reigns of power when...   *Religion/History/Biographies Pages 170*

The Complete Works of Guy de Maupassant by *Guy de Maupassant*   ISBN: *1-59462-157-8*   **$16.95**
"For days and days, nights and nights, I had dreamed of that first kiss which was to consecrate our engagement, and I knew not on what spot I should put my lips..."   *Fiction/Classics Pages 240*

The Art of Cross-Examination by *Francis L. Wellman*   ISBN: *1-59462-309-0*   **$26.95**
Written by a renowned trial lawyer, Wellman imparts his experience and uses case studies to explain how to use psychology to extract desired information through questioning.   *How-to/Science/Reference Pages 408*

Answered or Unanswered? by *Louisa Vaughan*   ISBN: *1-59462-248-5*   **$10.95**
Miracles of Faith in China
                                                                                                           Religion Pages 112

The Edinburgh Lectures on Mental Science (1909) by *Thomas*   ISBN: *1-59462-008-3*   **$11.95**
This book contains the substance of a course of lectures recently given by the writer in the Queen Street Hail, Edinburgh. Its purpose is to indicate the Natural Principles governing the relation between Mental Action and Material Conditions...   *New Age/Psychology Pages 148*

Ayesha by *H. Rider Haggard*   ISBN: *1-59462-301-5*   **$24.95**
Verily and indeed it is the unexpected that happens! Probably if there was one person upon the earth from whom the Editor of this, and of a certain previous history, did not expect to hear again...   *Classics Pages 380*

Ayala's Angel by *Anthony Trollope*   ISBN: *1-59462-352-X*   **$29.95**
The two girls were both pretty, but Lucy who was twenty-one who supposed to be simple and comparatively unattractive, whereas Ayala was credited, as her Bombwhat romantic name might show, with poetic charm and a taste for romance. Ayala when her father died was nineteen...   *Fiction Pages 484*

The American Commonwealth by *James Bryce*   ISBN: *1-59462-286-8*   **$34.45**
An interpretation of American democratic political theory. It examines political mechanics and society from the perspective of Scotsman James Bryce
                                                                                                        Politics Pages 572

Stories of the Pilgrims by *Margaret P. Pumphrey*   ISBN: *1-59462-116-0*   **$17.95**
This book explores pilgrims religious oppression in England as well as their escape to Holland and eventual crossing to America on the Mayflower, and their early days in New England...   *History Pages 268*

QTY

The Fasting Cure *by Sinclair Upton*　ISBN: *1-59462-222-1*　**$13.95**
In the Cosmopolitan Magazine for May, 1910, and in the Contemporary Review (London) for April, 1910, I published an article dealing with my experiences in fasting. I have written a great many magazine articles, but never one which attracted so much attention... New Age/Self Help/Health Pages 164　☐

Hebrew Astrology *by Sepharial*　ISBN: *1-59462-308-2*　**$13.45**
In these days of advanced thinking it is a matter of common observation that we have left many of the old landmarks behind and that we are now pressing forward to greater heights and to a wider horizon than that which represented the mind-content of our progenitors... Astrology Pages 144　☐

Thought Vibration or The Law of Attraction in the Thought World　ISBN: *1-59462-127-6*　**$12.95**

by William Walker Atkinson　*Psychology/Religion Pages 144*　☐

Optimism *by Helen Keller*　ISBN: *1-59462-108-X*　**$15.95**
Helen Keller was blind, deaf, and mute since 19 months old, yet famously learned how to overcome these handicaps, communicate with the world, and spread her lectures promoting optimism. An inspiring read for everyone... Biographies/Inspirational Pages 84　☐

Sara Crewe *by Frances Burnett*　ISBN: *1-59462-360-0*　**$9.45**
In the first place, Miss Minchin lived in London. Her home was a large, dull, tall one, in a large, dull square, where all the houses were alike, and all the sparrows were alike, and where all the door-knockers made the same heavy sound... Childrens/Classic Pages 88　☐

The Autobiography of Benjamin Franklin *by Benjamin Franklin*　ISBN: *1-59462-135-7*　**$24.95**
The Autobiography of Benjamin Franklin has probably been more extensively read than any other American historical work, and no other book of its kind has had such ups and downs of fortune. Franklin lived for many years in England, where he was agent... Biographies/History Pages 332　☐

Name	
Email	
Telephone	
Address	
City, State ZIP	

☐ **Credit Card**　　☐ **Check / Money Order**

Credit Card Number	
Expiration Date	
Signature	

Please Mail to:　Book Jungle
PO Box 2226
Champaign, IL 61825
or Fax to:　*630-214-0564*

ORDERING INFORMATION

web*: www.bookjungle.com*
email*: sales@bookjungle.com*
fax*: 630-214-0564*
mail*: Book Jungle PO Box 2226 Champaign, IL 61825*
or PayPal *to sales@bookjungle.com*

Please contact us for bulk discounts

DIRECT-ORDER TERMS

**20% Discount if You Order
Two or More Books**
Free Domestic Shipping!
Accepted: Master Card, Visa,
Discover, American Express

www.ingramcontent.com/pod-product-compliance
Lightning Source LLC
Chambersburg PA
CBHW080506110426
42742CB00017B/3018